A SPECTRUM OF UNFREEDOM

The Natalie Zemon Davis Annual Lecture Series
at Central European University, Budapest

A Spectrum of Unfreedom

Captives and Slaves
in the Ottoman Empire

Leslie Peirce

Central European University Press

Budapest–New York

Published in 2021 by

Central European University Press
Nádor utca 9, H-1051 Budapest, Hungary
224 West 57th Street, New York NY 10019, USA
Tel: +36-1-327-3138 or 327-3000
E-mail: *ceupress@press.ceu.edu*
Website: *www.ceupress.com*

ISBN 978-963-386-399-2 (paperback)
ISBN 978-963-386-400-5 (pdf)
ISSN 1996-1197

LIBRARY OF CONGRESS CATALOGING-IN-PUBLICATION DATA

Names: Peirce, Leslie P., author.
Title: A spectrum of unfreedom : captives and slaves in the Ottoman empire
    / Leslie Peirce.
Description: Budapest ; New York : Central European University Press, 2021.
    | Series: Natalie Zemon Davis annual lectures series, 1996–1197 |
    Includes bibliographical references and index.
Identifiers: LCCN 2021015142 (print) | LCCN 2021015143 (ebook) | ISBN
    9789633863992 (paperback) | ISBN 9789633864005 (adobe pdf)
Subjects: LCSH: Slavery—Turkey—History. | Captivity—Turkey—History. |
    Turkey—History—Ottoman Empire, 1288-1918.
Classification: LCC HT1238 .P45 2021 (print) | LCC HT1238 (ebook) | DDC
    306.3/6209561—dc23
LC record available at https://lccn.loc.gov/2021015142
LC ebook record available at https://lccn.loc.gov/2021015143

Table of Contents

Preface

I met Natalie Zemon Davis in in 1987 when I was writing my dissertation in the Near Eastern Studies Department at Princeton. I was approaching the final draft when my adviser thought I should have some help from a gender historian. He picked up the phone and I was in Natalie's office within a matter of minutes. I had already admired Natalie Davis, having gone to a talk she gave in a church basement. She was to talk about the book she was then writing (*The Return of Martin Guerre*) as well as her participation in the French film of the story.[1] This was not the professor of my undergraduate days in the 1960s, when we wrote down what we were told in class (with the exception of some junior faculty). Natalie was excited and exciting, especially when she spoke about a scene in the film that she had pushed for—the peasant Martin's wife Bertrande reveals that she can sign her name. This was a whole new world of history writing, and I wanted to try it. Later, I learned how supportive Natalie could be of her students, especially perhaps the women (with a full-time job and a son, I needed a model of a working mother).

How honored I was then when Gábor Klaniczay invited me to give the Natalie Zemon Davis Lectures at Central European University. For one thing, the feedback I received from the audience (always including Natalie's insightful comments) was both inspiring and, practically speaking, most useful for this book. I am also grateful to Gábor for giving me the idea for the last chapter of the book. In addition, he was a wonderful guide to the city, reminding me why Budapest is one of my favorite cities.

I was also delighted to meet new colleagues as well as reunite with old ones, from both the Medieval Studies and History departments. It was stimulating to hear some of their graduate students discuss their current projects. It was another pleasure to meet and converse with Karen Stark, who interviewed me for CEU Medieval Radio.[2] Finally, I would also like to thank Csilla Dobos for her excellent stewardship of my visit; I would literally have been lost without her help and advice.

Chapter One

An Overview of Ottoman Slavery

No one interested in the history of the Ottoman empire can ignore the work of those who found themselves in various forms of bondage. Without their labor, the ruling regime could not have attained or maintained the strength and stature it enjoyed in early modern times. Likewise, across the empire, in cities, towns, and villages, captives were a common presence in the human landscape, performing diverse roles in local economies and societies.

This book looks at captives and their captors across a broad range, from elite servants who sustained the dynastic family to unnamed victims seized by petty brigands. The unfree existed at virtually every level of society. A large number of captives were made slaves—that is, persons legally owned by subjects of the empire who ranged across different social and economic classes. But there were others, literally countless, whose bondage did not conform with the expec-

1

tations spelled out in either Islamic or imperial law. To study only the category of "legal" slaves is to miss broader and more complex phenomena that reduced large numbers to servitude.

To illustrate this diversity, here are four scenarios in which free persons might plausibly be thrust into captivity:

- A local brigand in Anatolia and his accomplices kidnap girls and boys during a raid on a large village, whose crops and livestock they might also seize.
- Slave raiders operating in the northern Black Sea region abduct a number of peasant boys and sell them at one of the region's slave markets. They are transported to Ottoman domains, their fate now in the hands of local dealers.
- A slave dealer sells a young woman at auction in a local slave market. A female buyer of moderate means might bid for her to help with domestic chores, or a male buyer acquire her for domestic labor and maybe to also serve as his concubine.
- A youth taken captive when his Serbian town refuses to surrender to victorious Ottoman forces is assessed for his capabilities and placed in preparatory training for the Janissary infantry corps, a prestigious unit in the imperial military.

The name of only the third captive was likely to appear in the historical record. The reason was that sales and purchases of humans were often entered in the registers of local law courts. If the Janissary apprentice had the rare good fortune to rise in the ranks and attain a position of command, his name might appear in a military record, for example, a salary or appointment register. Thankfully for historians, the Ottomans became assiduous keepers of registers of all sorts following the conquest in 1453 of Byzantine Constantinople and the subsequent consolidation of their domains into an empire. However, what has survived over the centuries to be studied by scholars may be only a fraction of the original handiwork of the empire's scribes. The fortunes of many captives—in all likelihood a considerable majority—are lost to history, especially the fate of those unnamed victims whose captors themselves are invisible.

In early modern times, the Ottomans drew on a sizable and sometimes imprecise and overlapping vocabulary for those in bondage—prisoner, servant, bondsman, prisoner of war, for example, in addition to numerous terms for slave. For this reason, it is useful to regard captivity as a spectrum of unfree persons. This book addresses the diversity and ambiguity of status by focusing on three categories of the unfree: "legal" slaves in domestic service across the empire;

the invisible victims of seizure by raiders, bandits, and the like; and, to a lesser degree, the *kul*, slaves in service to the Ottoman dynastic household.

* * *

The geography of captive-taking shifted over time. Most who would become slaves were seized from regions beyond Ottoman borderlands. These zones included Balkan lands, Greece, the Adriatic coast, Mediterranean islands and port cities, as well as regions north and east of the Black Sea. Others came from Egypt, today's Sudan, and Ethiopia. A small minority, with more distant origins such as India, were sold by their traveling owners in Ottoman slave markets.[1] The effect of this polyglot array was to funnel continuous variety into the already diverse Ottoman population.

This map of captive-taking is provided by "legal slaves"—those whose owners would take care to register them with local authorities. Country or region of origin was one of the standard identifiers that were inscribed in records, along with name, age, and physical features. In 1541, at the court of the southeastern Anatolian city of Aintab (today, Gaziantep), a member of the locally distinguished Sekkak family registered the sale of two female slaves to a sergeant stationed in the fortress of Maraş (today, Kahramanmaraş), the regional capital to the north. The first was described as a "thirteen-year-old slave girl by the name of Selvareh, of Georgian origin, light complected," and the second as "a child of eight, by the name of Harireh, of Ethiopian origin." (Harireh's physical appearance was presumably omitted because it had not yet taken sufficiently mature form.)[2] In Üsküdar, a borough of Istanbul on the Asian shore of the Bosphorus Strait, a runaway male slave of Russian origin was described as being of medium height, blond, open browed, and sparsely bearded; the red cap and white kaftan he reportedly wore were additional aids to his capture.[3]

The wide-ranging origins of captives help us trace the direction and timing of the Ottomans' territorial expansion, from their modest origins around 1300 in northeastern Anatolia to world empire by the mid-sixteenth century. When a new territory was invaded or conquered, local males were frequently taken as prisoners of war and women and children seized as war booty. The earliest captives came from neighboring Byzantine lands and then, as Ottoman forces moved into the Balkans, from Thrace, and then from the region of Macedonia and Bulgaria. Serbia was yielding victims by the end of the fourteenth century,[4] followed by Bosnia and Albania.[5] Captives from Serbia can furnish an example of this serial expansion: their numbers peaked around

1454, while by 1484 they ranked eighth among beleaguered nations; numbers soon dwindled as other populations became more accessible or desirable.

By the early 1490s, Ottoman victories along the western and northern Black Sea coasts facilitated an influx of Slavic-speaking captives from what is today's Ukraine and southern Russia (they were known commonly as *Rus*). By the 1540s or so, numbers of black slaves from eastern African territories could be found in Üsküdar, Aintab, and elsewhere. Some of them were likely to have been purchased by travelers to Mecca and Medina, where the annual pilgrimage furnished opportunities for trade in humans.[6] Around 1500, corsair warfare on and around the shores of the Mediterranean began to furnish captives from North Africa and southern Europe (captives taken from Ottoman lands went in the reverse direction).[7]

One useful map of the diverse origins of captives in the early sixteenth century is furnished by a document that lists the homelands of male kul who served Suleyman I during his princely apprenticeship in the western Anatolian city of Manisa. The population of select young men in training for the elite military and governing class numbered fifty-six, thirty-three of whose origins were listed: seven Albanians, ten Croatians, three Bosnians, one Serbian, three Rus, six Circassians, one Georgian, and two Abkhazians.[8]

* * *

Like their varied origins, the conditions under which
captives lived occupied a broad spectrum, from the
relative comfort enjoyed by the skilled (generally well
treated because of their monetary value) to conditions
of abject servitude suffered by others. Much depended
on the stature of one's owner. The sergeant in Maraş
paid a total of 3,000 silver aspers for the slave girls
Selvareh and Harireh, an expense that was beyond
the means of most individuals living in the provinces of which Aintab and Maraş were the capitals. In
1526 the average annual household tax amounted to
240 aspers, while in the poorer province of Maraş it
was 168 aspers. (At the time, two aspers was a typical daily allotment for the upkeep of an orphan child,
a divorced wife, a runaway slave in detention, or a
stray animal waiting to be claimed by its owner.)[9]

Ownership of slaves was not necessarily confined
to the well-to-do. An individual of limited means
may have lived only a degree or two more comfort-
ably than his or her servant. Such was the situation of
the farmer Hasan, who lived in a semi-rural suburb
of Istanbul. While the monetary value of his material possessions at his death—200 aspers—was somewhat larger than the average of his fellow villagers, his
house was described as little more than a shed with an

attached stable. Apparently valuing productivity over comfort, Hasan owned a slave worth 1,800 aspers.[10]

The domestic establishments of wealthy Ottoman subjects, by contrast, typically housed a range of both female and male slaves who varied from menial workers to the highly skilled. The latter attended upon their owners and applied their talents when so commanded—females might entertain their mistress's guests with music and dance, for example, and male apprentices might carry out transactions in their master or mistress's name. These elite slaves arrived with or could be trained in a wide range of expertise. It is hard to say what percentage had the opportunity or the know-how to improve their skills and therefore their lot in life, but it is clear that slavery offered upward mobility for some at least.

Foremost among elite establishments was the sultanate, the premier household of the empire. In reference to the Ottoman dynasty, the term "household" encompasses more than royal residences, for it included all those who served at the sultan's command. They too were known as *kul,* one of the several words for slave. In addition to the hundreds of kul who worked and lived in the imperial palaces in Istanbul and elsewhere, the sultan's household counted top military forces of the empire: generals and their lieutenants as well as the soldier-statesmen who served the empire as provincial governors and, at the pinnacle, the sultan's viziers.

The imperial harem must also be counted as a kul institution. Housed in the "Old Palace," separate from the sultan's "New Palace," it numbered several hundred females, some of them members of the dynasty. Well-trained female slaves were groomed for personal service to the sultan himself, his family members, and his high-ranking concubines. Eunuch slaves served as guardians of the women as well as intermediaries with the outside world; in the late fifteenth century, a corps of black eunuchs emerged in the inner quarters of the sultan's palace. John Sanderson, secretary to the English embassy at the end of the sixteenth century, estimated kul numbers in Istanbul at 81,200 out of a total population of 1,231,207.[11]

Other thousands of kul were stationed throughout the empire—on its frontiers, in its strategic urban areas, and in large numbers of its villages. The captive Serbian youth imagined above would have begun his Ottoman life in the corps of the *acemi oğlan*, "novice boys" (actually, teenagers who had first been placed with Turkish farmers to learn the language and adapt to hard labor). If the novice showed aptitude, he might be promoted to the Janissary corps. The circumstance of low-level recruits, however, could be pitiable. An early seventeenth-century treatise calling for Janissary reform lamented that novice boys worked barefoot and bare-headed while carrying sacks of earth and stone for the construction of Sultan Suleyman's great mosque, until his wife Hurrem allegedly persuaded him to raise their salaries.[12] (Suleyman's favorite slave concubine, Hurrem became a powerful figure when he broke precedent by freeing and marrying her.)

Due to their ubiquitous presence in one capacity or another, the kul appear in various places and capacities throughout the chapters of this book. Its principal focus, however, is the slaves taken in warfare and the nameless captives seized within the empire's borders.

* * *

Popular history of the later fifteenth century imagined that the early Ottoman sultans fostered an egalitarian society, with Osman, first in the dynastic lineage, living the frugal life of a frontier pastoralist. This picture is belied by the sophistication of his son Orhan's household: in the year of his father's death, it already bore the trappings of a notable establishment. It boasted, for example, a eunuch who managed a charitable foundation Orhan had established (eunuchs broadcast status, as they were expensive slaves). When the famous Moroccan traveler Ibn Battuta visited the Ottoman capital of Bursa in 1331, seven years after Osman's death, he remarked that Orhan's was the richest of the several Turkish principalities in Anatolia.

Princes learned from one another. The early Ottomans borrowed from the Byzantines whom they ultimately displaced. They could also learn from their fellow Turkish lords, who would eventually fall one by one to Orhan's successors. In turn, the dynasty's practice of creative emulation had a trickle-down effect, as numerous local magnates in urban centers across the empire adopted fashions emanating from imperial Istanbul. It is no surprise that the slave populations of these great provincial households also occupied a wide range of status and function.[13] It has been said of seventeenth-century Aleppo, for example, that its elite households "organized human resources on a medium to large scale in efforts to preserve their material assets and project their influence."[14] The proliferation of large households and enterprises that created demand for staffs of slaves was in considerable part the outcome of the prosperity generated by the *Pax Ottomanica*—the stabilizing effect of a large empire in its heyday.

Like the dynastic regime, elite households throughout the empire engaged the labor not only of slaves but also of former slaves who had earned their freedom. Abu Taqiyya, a prominent merchant of Cairo, employed his own freed slaves as stewards of the goods he purveyed along trading networks from Venice to ports on the Red Sea; his former Ethiopian slave, Haji Hamdun, passed away in the Yemeni port of Mocha on one such trip.[15] When, in 1613, Abu Taqiyya acquired the powerful post of head of the Cairo merchant guild, he expanded his and his wives' domicile accordingly through the purchase of the mansion next door to their own. In addition to doubled courtyards, great halls, and loggias, the compound now included a stable, a bathhouse, a mill, and two storerooms.[16] The number of slaves and freed slaves necessary to maintain both the operation of the dual mansions and the prestige of the family was doubtless considerable.

There were other reasons than household reputation for staffing large numbers of slaves. For one, purchasing a slave could be a form of investment. The training imparted by owners added to the value that could be recouped if and when the slave was resold. Another advantage to slave ownership was that it offered freedom from fluctuations in the human labor market, where limited supply or seasonal migration might hamper production. Slaves could also function as a kind of ready cash, as they did for the scion of the Sekkak family in Aintab who sold the two young slave girls. He had fallen into dire financial straits and was under arraignment for debts he owed to the Ottoman government.

It was not only the domestic labor slaves performed that made them essential to certain classes but also the prestige that their owners derived from possessing wealth in human form. When men and women of the elites went into public arenas, their choice slaves would form a retinue escorting them, the purpose of which was to broadcast the family's social standing and sometimes its political importance. Other cultures might measure status by the grandeur of one's residence—to which Ottomans certainly attended—but the numbers of attendants accompanying one into public space registered one's status more immediately and memorably.

This point was made clear in a series of fatwas issued by Ebu Suud, mufti of Istanbul from 1545 to his death in 1574. He was apparently queried frequently for his opinion on what qualified a female for the honorific appellation *muhaddere*—honorable, of sound reputation. Perhaps wishing to head off more such queries, Ebu Suud issued a detailed answer underlining the point that female respectability was not a matter of Islamic piety (ruling on which was a mufti's charge). "It is not conformity to the prescriptions of the noble Sharia that is the essential element in being muhaddere," he emphasized. "That is why Jewish and Christian women can also be muhaddere. A woman is muhaddere if she does not let herself be seen by males [outside the immediate family] and does not set about taking care of her affairs in person."[17] The assumption was that muhaddere women had slaves to manage public aspects of their business.

To clarify this interpretation of the law, the mufti provided rules of conduct in shorter fatwas: a village woman who fetched water at the well could not be muhaddere, but a woman who was escorted by a retinue to a bathhouse, a wedding, or another neighborhood could. In other words, the retinue, comprised of slaves, was the key to an elite woman's ability to appear on public streets and avenues. Males required no such justification for their presence in public, but a distinguished man took care to announce his status with the size of his own retinue. People necessarily made way for the entourages of distinguished individuals. Ottoman miniature paintings of the period suggest that they were also eager spectators, lining the streets as Londoners do for royal weddings. The sultan naturally employed the largest retinue by far and drew the largest crowds of onlookers.

* * *

The perennial demand for unfree labor by the Ottoman sultanate and its subjects stemmed from a number of factors and developments that accompanied the

14

transformation of a small regional power into a burgeoning empire on three continents. There were rules regarding who could be deprived of his or her freedom. Islamic law held that a Muslim could not enslave another Muslim. Furthermore, Christian and Jewish subjects of a Muslim sovereign were by law protected peoples and thus also off limits to slavers (although they were subject to special taxes and other restrictions that Muslims were not). In theory, enslavement could therefore only take place beyond Ottoman borders, in the so-called Domain of War. There, prisoners could legitimately be taken if their city, region, or kingdom resisted surrender to victorious Ottoman forces.

These rules were not always honored, however, especially when the demand for manpower and womanpower outpaced supply. The first Ottomans had got their start as raiders, and even as formal military units developed, volunteer raiders were not stopped from kidnapping humans—indeed, they were often encouraged to do so. The late fifteenth-century chronicler Aşıkpaşazade, an enthusiast of Ottoman conquest, recalled a foray across the Danube which yielded so many captives that raiders were selling girls "for the price of a boot."[18] The Serbian soldier Konstantin Mihailović, who served Mehmed II "the Conqueror" between 1455 and 1463, observed that "the Turks capture people, not livestock. . . . Having taken [captives] they swiftly ride away with them. . . . And the more men you maintain, wanting to prevent this, the greater the expense and torment you will bear."[19]

Even Christian subjects of the empire, whose free status was guaranteed by law, could find themselves conscripted into kul service. (Jewish subjects, generally urban dwellers and often entrepreneurs, were apparently more valuable for their taxes and their trading networks.) The rationale for transgressing the protected status of Ottoman Christians was the exigencies of empire—*maslahat*, raison d'état—especially the frequent shortages of manpower.

Known as the *devshirme*, "gathering" or "collection," the draft of Christian subjects was controversial in its own times. The scholar and government servant Idris Bitlisi, who served Selim I (d. 1520), endorsed the practice on the grounds that most of these captives were the property of the sultan, and it was right to employ them as fighters in a Holy War and to carry out decrees of the administration. In contrast, Mustafa 'Ali, writing at the end of the century and likewise a savant cum government functionary, believed the *devshirme* was no longer justifiable and its agents "tyrannical." The former wrote during the heyday of conquest, while Mustafa 'Ali's views were formed when Ottoman domains were no longer expanding as rapidly as before and the flow of captives slowed.[20] 'Ali's critique may also reflect a rise in domestic slavery and the demands it made on the commerce in slaves.

In addition to the market for domestic slaves, the military establishment generated its own demand for slave power. The Ottoman dislike of hired mercenary corps meant that the sultanate maintained a substantial army, whose largest contingent was the cavalry. It was composed principally of captive Christian converts, as was the Janissary infantry corps. Typically stationed across the empire in the villages and small towns of its provinces, cavalrymen were assigned grants of income from the revenues of their posts, which were known as *timars*. The timariot's job in peacetime was to keep order, ensure payment of taxes, and generally promote local welfare. In wartime, however, a percentage of provincial timariots were mobilized, with those possessing large timars required to bring along one or more recruits outfitted for combat. Because peasants and townsmen—free tax-paying subjects—were off limits, captives were logical candidates for a timariot's entourage. In 1431, Mustafa, an Albanian convert to Islam and a timariot with a handsome revenue, was required in wartime to furnish two armed men, a slave-servant, a standard tent, and a lean-to tent.[21]

Captive-taking enriched not only the empire's fighting forces but also its treasury. The state claimed one in every five prisoners taken in combat or seized as booty. The *pençik* ("one in five"), as it was known, could alternately take the form of a monetary payment by the captor. The levy varied: in late fifteenth-century Bursa (the first city taken by the Ottomans in 1326 and a major entrepôt for buying and selling slaves), an infant's pençik ranged from 10 to 30 silver aspers, while a healthy male adolescent's value could be as much as 250 to 280 aspers.[22] Elsewhere the pençik was apparently less well regulated, prompting Sultan Bayezid II (d. 1512) to systematize it.

There is no doubt that that the Ottoman sultanate encouraged captive-taking. It regularly used the incentive of human as well as material booty to make its military campaigns more robust. To prepare for the critical effort in 1484 to annex two port cities on the Black Sea's northwest rim, Bayezid II issued a call to arms. He ordered judges in the empire's provincial centers to broadcast it to potential fighters. Volunteer raiders were likely a particular target:

Let them come with their weapons of war and their battle gear and join me in this blessed holy war so that they might find satisfaction [lit. satiety] in booty and gain riches in plunder. And let each one who participates earn from me esteem and favors to the degree of his participation. Let me favor and reward with timars . . . those who aspire to [gain] them. May they be acknowledged and delighted by my royal favors. (Akgündüz, *Kanunlar*, II: 135)

In addition to promising timars to civilians, the call to arms also announced that the pençik would not be imposed that year and that the troops "should act accordingly"—in other words, take all the captives they could manage. The campaign was a success, cementing Ottoman dominance in the Black Sea and facilitating the transport of grain and other foodstuffs to the imperial capital.[23]

Meanwhile, free subjects of the sultanate were falling vulnerable to the imposition of non-military forms of captivity. This danger was particularly evident following the conquest of Constantinople in 1453 and the refurbishment of the much-wasted city. Mehmed the Conqueror attempted to repopulate the new Ottoman capital by offering incentives. The upshot of successful urban resettlement, however, was the greater number of mouths to feed in the expanding capital. A perennial concern over the centuries, the provisioning of Istanbul was a particularly acute worry following the conquest, and it too was answered by the forced labor of male subjects of the sultan.

Establishing new farming communities on uncultivated or abandoned land was one of those exigencies of state. Despite the fact that the law forbad the up-rooting of the free peasantry, Mehmed the Conqueror answered the need for agricultural workers by trans-planting peasants from the empire's European territo-ries to 160 state-owned villages in the capital's vicinity. Scholars have described these "repatriated" workers as slaves, serfs, and/or sharecroppers.[24] The practice of forcible transfer of populations (*sürgün*) would be em-ployed not only to transport talent where it was criti-cally needed but also to expel rebellious or otherwise troublesome groups from their home base. Inhabit-ants of European provinces would be relocated to ter-ritories in Asia and vice versa. The practice of *sürgün* was indispensable to the survival of the Ottoman pol-ity, from its start to its end six centuries later. These displaced persons were not all slaves, but it is fair to say that they were hostage to the state.

It is clear that the supply of captives frequently lagged behind both the needs and wants of the Otto-man state and society. This was particularly evident as the empire's expansion slowed down in the later six-teenth century. Stoking the perennial demand was a growing appetite for slaves, perhaps even a sense of entitlement to ownership. The Ottomans were hardly alone as assiduous captors, however. Corsairs of varied origins and loyalties plied the Mediterranean Sea, and by 1545, Turks, Greeks, and Moors were manning the galleys of Marseille.[25] This mutual thieving of foreign populations inspired ransom efforts and sometimes prisoner swaps around its shores.[26] (The Qur'an cites ransoming prisoners as one of the legitimate uses of religious tithing, testimony to the long history of captive-taking in the region.)[27] On the Hungarian–Ottoman frontier, a virtual industry of ransom and prisoner exchange was sustained, and it was not always clear who was taking advantage of whom.[28]

It was not a universal assumption in these centuries that humans had an innate right to freedom or that they could assume protection from the monarch who ruled over (and taxed) them. Moreover, states were often bounded less by precise territorial borders than by frontiers that might fluctuate between adversaries. Such ambiguous borderlands could be ripe picking grounds for captives.

* * *

There was one source of ongoing demand for slaves that arose more from a humanitarian than a military, social, or economic impetus. The Qur'an encouraged Muslims to free their slaves, and over the centuries manumission became widely regarded as a meritorious act. There were enough members of early modern Ottoman society who observed this moral injunction

21

to generate a steady market for the "replacement" purchase of slaves.

The motivations of mistresses and masters who voluntarily freed their slaves included piety, repentance, and sometimes an oath they had taken. Acts of manumission were often registered in local courts, the rationale that the former slave's new status was now validated by the court record dictated by the judge (*kadı*). In addition, this inscription of the manumission memorialized the former owner's performance of a good deed. Local Ottoman courts acted as notaries as well as forums for litigation, and it was a requirement that virtually every proceeding be witnessed by upstanding male residents of the judge's jurisdiction. The outcome was that reputable members of the local community were additional repositories of the "legal memory" of this critical change in a former slave's status. Freeing a slave could thus be a public act lodged in communal memory.

Instances of manumission recorded by provincial judges provide a sense of the process of freeing one's slave. In 1540, Mehmed, member of the Hundarlu tribe, petitioned the Aintab court to provide a certificate of freedom (*ıtkname*) for Abidin, a black slave his father had freed; the father had willed that Mehmed obtain the court's validation on behalf of the new freedman.[29] Abidin's was a typical instance of the form of emancipation known as *tedbir* (lit. "precaution," "foresight"): the freeing of a slave at the death of the owner who had previously registered (or in this case performed) his or her intent, often during old age or illness.

Tedbir manumission had the virtue of exempting the slave from being counted in the deceased's inheritable estate and thereby an object of possible contention among the heirs. Perhaps the two brothers in late sixteenth-century Ankara who pledged in court to free their slave Mercan at the end of one year were elderly and engaged in estate planning. Three days after the brothers' appearance, the Ankara court register noted that another man who had freed a slave on the occasion of his son's circumcision was now requesting that a manumission certificate be drawn up.[30]

Things could go wrong with vows, particularly those made spontaneously. The case of Mehmed Çelebi, a fabric merchant in Manisa, concerned a vow to free his slaves that backfired on him. Confronted by a customer for whom he had mistakenly packaged up the wrong coat, Mehmed refused to acknowledge the buyer's protest. He retained a modicum of credibility, however, by swearing that he would free all his slaves, female and male, if he were proven wrong—which he soon was. Although Mehmed acknowledged his error, he still refused to honor his vow. Two of his slaves—Ahmed and a woman called Gülşah—

took him to court and won their freedom.[31] In other words, the failure to honor a vow was legally actionable by a slave—at least in the Manisa court.

Vows made in the heat of the moment were apparently commonplace, despite their often unintended and painful outcomes. A habit among men, for example, was to swear "If I ever do such-and-such, may my wife be triply [definitively] divorced." These hasty dissolutions of family unity were rife around the mid-sixteenth century, as demonstrated by the numbers of fatwas clarifying the status of a dissolved marriage. One wonders if Ahmed and Gülşah had boned up on the law? Maybe so, though it was not unusual that ordinary individuals could be aware of basic legal principles. Numerous precepts embedded in Ottoman law were so ancient and ingrained in the broad region of the Near East that people sometimes seemed to intuit their rights.

On the other hand, the victory of the fabric merchant's slaves should not necessarily suggest that agents of the law routinely stepped up to defend mistreated slaves. Factors that influenced the quality of justice included the stature of the slave's owner in the local hierarchy of power and the slave's degree of proximity to a legal authority. Ahmed and Gülşah had the advantage of access to the judge of Manisa, one of the handful of regional capitals in Anatolia where Ottoman princes were sent to learn the arts of ruling.

Wherever there was an imperial presence, there was likely to be a well-functioning court.

Residents of Manisa and its hinterland villages had the additional option, in theory at least, of bringing their grievances directly to the resident prince. Like the caliphs and sultans whose polities preceded them, Ottoman rulers upheld the principle that subjects had the right to petition the monarch directly. To be sure, face-to-face access waned as Ottoman dynasts adopted the protocols of imperial distancing practiced by Byzantine emperors and Abbasid caliphs before them. The result was that petitioning the ruler, or rather the delegates of his authority, gradually became a more elaborate bureaucratic process. Nevertheless, the principle of the right to imperial justice endured. (Chapter 2 makes use of petitions to the reigning sultan that originated in a variety of provincial communities.)

The ability and willingness of slaves to stand up for themselves in the face of abuse by their owners doubtless varied. The bold and assertive had a better chance, as did those who could be confident that local arbiters—the judge, a mufti, a well-regarded figure in the neighborhood, perhaps a supportive freed person—might take their side or at least listen to their plight. Local cultural practices of course played a critical role, as did the slave's familiarity with the law. A dispute between a female owner in Üsküdar and her newly freed female slave Gülbahar demonstrates the resourcefulness of the latter. When her mistress proceeded to sell her for 2,500 aspers, Gülbahar, who was in possession of her manumission certificate, challenged and won her suit. She helped her own case by noting that it was illegal to sell a Muslim. Like the preponderance of slaves of Muslim owners, she had been converted to Islam.

Üsküdar was a district of cosmopolitan Istanbul with its own court. Living at the heart of the empire, its slaves were more likely to have access to legal expertise and assistance than those in provincial locales. The various regions of the empire, moreover, had evolved different practices and assumptions over centuries that predated the coming of the Ottoman legal regime. And, like women or peasants from remote villages, other populations might hold back from using the courts. The fortunes of black slaves, at least in Aintab, could be precarious, as two cases suggest. In both, however, the accused were protected by the provincial court itself.

The first case concerns an apparent instance of mistaken identity. Having alleged that the slave Abdullah stole his three donkeys, the accuser later admitted in court that he had the wrong black man. (The culprit turned out to be one Mubarek who already had a criminal record.) In a routine procedure, residents of the village where Abdullah lived were summoned to court as character witnesses: they testified that "this black [man] is a trustworthy person, we have never observed any wrongdoing on his part, he is an honest young man."[32]

In the second case, the slave Saʿid confessed to a murder but then proceeded to testify that his master's brother had forced him to carry out the deed. The understanding between them had been that the brother would take responsibility if Saʿid was accused. Unfortunately, the court register does not record the settlement of this affair. While judges tried cases, it was provincial governors and their delegates who meted out punishment for crimes of violence for which public records did not exist in early modern times. Fortunately, a fatwa issued by Ebu Suud addressed Saʿid's situation: the mufti ruled that a master who ordered a killing should be sentenced to "a long imprisonment," while the slave must pay the requisite blood money to the family of the slain.[33] A fatwa issued by the empire's chief mufti was likely to address a common occurrence.

* * *

Once manumitted, freed persons sometimes had to struggle to protect their new status. For one thing, losing one's certificate of manumission seems to have been a fairly common misfortune. If a slave was far from the place where he had been manumitted, proof of his free status might be difficult to obtain swiftly. Such was the situation of a freed Russian slave recorded at the Ankara court. He was turned over to the office that housed runaway slaves, stray or stolen animals, and others in limbo. The judge allotted a daily stipend for the Russian's maintenance to support him while he attempted to rectify his situation.[34]

Another liability that apparently plagued the freed person was being mistaken for a slave, or so the relative frequency of such incidents suggests. The loss of manumission certificates becomes understandable if freedmen felt the necessity to carry their papers on their person whenever they left their local environment. Slave women didn't seem to lose their certificates, but then their labor did not take them far from their owner's home or place of business.

For some slaves, the route to manumission was built into the nature of their labor. A prime example is the slave concubine mother of a free Muslim man's child. By Islamic law she was freed upon his death, while during his lifetime she could not be sold or given away. The relative frequency of concubinage owed much to the rule that the children of such a union were born free, unless the father were to deny paternity (a situation that is not readily apparent in sources of the period.) These stipulations have led some to assert that more female than male slaves thereby gained their freedom.

The social status of slave concubines was boosted by the fact that Muslim monarchs from the Abbasid caliphate forward often chose concubines to be the mothers of their heirs. As for the Ottomans, from the fifteenth century onward, sultans and princes reproduced exclusively with slave concubines from beyond Ottoman borders, the more powerful of whom left their mark on history. A principal rationale for this policy was to forestall political interference by the foreign powers who had provided princess brides in earlier centuries. Such threats had troubled the sultanate in the era of its expansion and development.

This did not mean that royal concubines were lesser consorts—they may have had no family pedigrees, but they were politically more consequential as royal mothers. Moreover, having been converted to Islam, they could make a lasting name for themselves through philanthropic donations. This status of royal mothers apparently emboldened some ordinary slave women to refuse marriage to male slaves. The impact of such balking could be seen in the plight of unmarried men who had been drafted to work in the villages Mehmed the Conqueror established for the provisioning of Istanbul. One outcome, reported by a government inspector in 1498, was a decrease in the slave population.[35]

Another class of slaves who could expect to become free was known as *mükatebe,* a classification that approximates contract worker. The relationship between the slave and the master or mistress was a negotiated one. The terms of the contract that set out the slave's obligation could vary: a specified number of years of service, a set quota of goods produced, or a set monetary value of goods produced. The verb *kesmek,* "to cut," was typically employed in negotiations with the meaning "to cut a deal," that is, to come to a contractual agreement.

In Ankara for example, registering mükatebe arrangements seems to have been routine. The court record from November 1588 to July 1590 notes that the Rus slave Ferhad negotiated a ten-year contract, and Veli Bey bargained to free his slave Şirmerd after fifteen years of service.[36] (Apparently either party could initiate court registration of the contract, at least in Ankara.) An example of a wage-based contract drawn up at the court was that of the slave Kasım, engaged by his master for 120 aspers a month. By contrast, the court of Aintab, a province with substantial commerce in woven and other manufactured goods and presumably employers of mükatebe slaves, was apparently not a forum for recording such negotiations. This variation underlines the fact that different regions with different legal histories employed their courts for different purposes. The Ottoman empire was a checkerboard of legal as well as economic and political cultures.

Mükatebe workers could be found in a variety of hired occupations—in Üsküdar, for example, an oarsman or a foreman on a grain-producing farm. Üsküdar was best known, however, for its participation in the craft and manufacturing sectors of the Ottoman economy. The luxury textile industry of Bursa is perhaps the most widely known example of the employment of highly skilled workers. The contract of the velvet weaver Özeyir, a slave from Venice, called for 120 embroidered pieces to be completed, while the Bosnian woman Kumri's contract stipulated a payment of 5,000 dirhams for 50 pieces of silk gauze.[37] Experienced and trusted male slaves could be employed in a mükatebe arrangement as their owner's agent in long-distance trade. In sum, it is fair to say that the most accomplished contract workers constituted an elite class of slaves, performing for the economy what the upper echelons of the kul did for Ottoman dynastic rule. They have been described as licensed slaves, carrying out their masters and mistresses' business in public.[38]

Despite their seemingly elite status, mükatebe slaves were not necessarily shielded from abuse by their owners. In the mid-fifteenth century, in the town of Ermeni Pazarı, a slave named Nikola appeared at court. His complaint, as phrased in the record, was the following:

> My master and I agreed on a term of seven years. Now the seven years are fulfilled. He is oppressing me and does not let me have my letter of emancipation. It is necessary now that an order be given for him to carry out the agreement.

"Oppression" was a catchword that was employed frequently in sixteenth and seventeenth-century petitions to the sultan when subjects wanted to underline the severity of the abuse they were suffering at the hands of superiors. Nikola's legal fluency makes one wonder if slaves with grievances were coached by their more experienced coworkers or how often professional scribes translated petitioners' unsophisticated statements into the proper formulaic language.

Emancipation did not bring instant integration into free society. Rather than moving directly into a state of freedom, manumitted slaves typically first occupied the transitional state of freed person (*'atik/ 'atika*). Just when the progeny of a freed slave was accepted as freeborn is not clear—in fact, it may not have been uniform across time and place. It has been asserted for late fifteenth-century Bursa that the standard patronymic identifying a Muslim slave—*Ibn Abdullah*, "son of the slave of God"; *Bint Abdullah* for females—was not applied to the offspring of a freedperson; in other words, the second generation was regarded as fully free. Elsewhere the slave patronymic was not dropped until the generation of the original slave's grandsons and granddaughters. Again, variation was presumably the effect of varying cultures and social or economic practices as well as the degree of familiarity with slaves and freedpersons in a particular city or region. Bursa was an area long familiar with the presence of slaves.

The relationship between former owner and freedperson often continued. Perhaps as compensation for the interim status of *'atik*, masters and mistresses were enjoined to ease the passage of manumitted slaves into free adult society. Most typical was helping them establish a marital household by identifying a compatible mate and/or financing an appropriate residence. This practice also obtained in the imperial household: highly trained male and female kul were typically joined in marriage when they graduated from palace to public service. One of the charitable endeavors of the famous seventeenth-century queen mother Kösem emphasized the importance of helping those who lacked parents who would provide the means to marry. During the three holy months of the year, Kösem furnished dowries for orphaned girls. She would emerge from the palace incognito in order to identify worthy recipients of her aid.

The families of former owner and former slave might continue to be connected by ties of patronage and clientage, and freed persons might continue to work for their former owner. This was true of both "civilian" and imperial households: the eunuch who managed Sultan Orhan's charitable foundation was his freed former slave. One limitation to this relationship, however, was the fact that the former master or mistress retained certain legal claims over the estate of a former slave at his or her death—a situation that was not always straightforward and could lead to disagreement. At the death of Hasan, the Üsküdar farmer with the meager house and expensive slave, his modest assets revealed serious debt, leading to disputes over his estate. Hasan had been the freedman of a local landowner (himself deceased), and the slave ended up as the property of the landowner's son. An analogous pattern held true for the sultanate, which claimed the right to seize certain property of high-ranking kul at their death.

* * *

This chapter concludes with some comments on the challenges of understanding slavery among the early modern Ottomans. One is the difficulty of estimating the proportion of Ottoman subjects who rarely or never appeared before a judge. Slaves living in remote villages or among migratory tribes were less able than urban dwellers to bring their problems to court. Deputy judges might be sent out to more remote locales to investigate serious problems, but the ability of a slave to generate attention was limited. In sum, our "database" is only partially representative of the lives of slaves.

Secondly, knowledge regarding slaves is largely limited to documentary records that survived the wages of time (fire, flood, and general neglect). A significant move in the consolidation of imperial rule following the conquest of Constantinople was Mehmed II's repeated effort to induce local judges to treat registers of court proceedings as a public record—that is, to preserve them in a designated safe space (the sultan called for storing them in a chest). Traditionally, judges had retained the registers generated during their tenure, with the result that access could be difficult for those who needed to consult past cases relevant to current concerns.[39] This critical reform pushed by the sultan had the effect of redistributing authority, with the state and local legal experts now sharing jurisdiction.

Mehmed's successors continued to advance efforts to draw local courts into an empire-wide orbit of administration, with the aim of creating a more uniform legal practice across Ottoman domains. A core reform was the gradual replacement of judges of local origin by state-appointed ones, as had happened in in the provincial court of Aintab in 1541. It had apparently been customary practice for men of the province to discourage their wives, sisters, and even adult sons from bringing grievances to court. However, when the first state-appointed judge, Hüsameddin Efendi, was assigned to Aintab in 1541, things changed rather rapidly. The court soon began to see more clients, with a significant uptick in the numbers of women who came to register monetary transactions, for example, or appeal to the judge for redress.

It was not that the sultanate was pursuing an early-modern version of gender parity but rather that women were crucial figures in local societies, and the government wanted them under its legal scrutiny. Women's agency stemmed largely from their rights to independent control of their property, acquired principally through inheritance and marriage dower. These rights were based in traditional Islamic law, which judges and sultans alike were charged with enforcing. In addition, since legal procedure relied heavily on the testimony of witnesses, women's input could sometimes be essential to the resolution of a case.

The shift in 1541 in the court user population was not due only to the presence of the new judge. Suleyman I had recently issued an expanded compilation of sultanic law (*kanun*). He was the third and final sultan to do so following Mehmed II's initial issuing around 1480 of an imperial statute book (*Kanunname-i Osmani*). Hüsameddin Efendi apparently brought Suleyman's updated edition with him. It seems he also anticipated increased legal traffic, for soon after his arrival the court venue was expanded in size, with the result that it was now more accessible to the public. Women, for instance, could be accompanied by family elders, thereby preserving their reputations. It is not coincidental that Suleyman earned the regnal sobriquet "Kanunî," the lawgiver, the just.

Despite the general effectiveness of imperial efforts to standardize and popularize the Ottoman court system, variation in local legal traditions inevitably persisted in such an extensive and variegated polity. In theory, a judge could be rotated from a post in Bulgaria to eastern Anatolia and then to Cairo, each locale presenting different economic and cultural features (respectively, farming, tribal pastoralism, urban entrepreneurship). Judges had to be flexible and ready to adapt to local conditions and legal habits. This necessity is underlined by the sources of law that shaped the testimony of court users and the decisions of judges. In addition to Sharia law and sultanic law, a third source was local customary law (*kanun-ı kadim*, `*adet*,). The repository of customary law was the collective knowledge of leading men of the province and—less often—females with particular expertise, such as midwives. These individuals could provide confirmation of long-standing patterns of behavior that enjoyed consensus among the provincial population.

Despite the efforts of both the sultanate and local communities, there are significant urban centers in former Ottoman lands that today lack a legal archive of the Ottoman era—whether through catastrophic events such as flood or fire, negligence in preserving court documents, or difficulties in maintaining a judge's court. But an even greater gap in our understanding of slavery is the paucity of information about captives who did not become legal slaves and were consequently rendered mute in the historical record. The next chapter explores their fates.

Chapter Two

Captives and Their Captors

While there were legal slaves whose identity and fate were unknown, the captives who populate this chapter are virtually invisible in the historical record. Countless numbers of individuals—male and female, adult and child—were seized from their homes and neighborhoods. The circumstances of their capture were sometimes recorded, but only rarely were their names. This reality is vividly evident in the many desperate appeals to the sultan's government for both protection and rescue efforts. How often families were successful in their own attempts to recover missing relatives and neighbors is difficult to determine.

As a consequence, the contours of captive lives are much less knowable than those of the slaves in chapter 1. By necessity, the primary focus of this chapter is the phenomenon of captive-taking, its causes, and the attempts to stop, or at least mitigate, its damaging outcomes. Playing principal roles in this history (apart from captors) are local authorities, government policy makers and enforcers, as well as the law itself in its formulations and implementations. Less present are the local populations who were intimidated by the violence of kidnappers.

The largest numbers of captives were victims of raids by brigands, petty outlaws, and, at times, even government functionaries. Victims were seized primarily from village homes and fields but also from small towns and, a particular menace, on open roads. Others were purchased on black markets operating outside official venues for the sale of slaves; there they might also be resold. While adult males could be targets of abduction, it was women, girls, and boys who were the primary victims. (Children were never cited collectively as victims, in part because both their social and legal status as victims differed.) From the late sixteenth century to the mid-seventeenth, when waves of internal discord broke out in Anatolia, local communities suffered increasing vulnerability. Captors had always included delegates of the sultan's authority, among them locally stationed soldiers and policing agents. Now, however, sundry servants of the sultanate such as commanders, governors, even judges, were becoming part of the problem.

Given the clandestine nature of captives' circumstances, the contours of their daily lives are largely a matter of conjecture. As with slaves, the fortunes of captives were linked to the status of their masters, thus, they likely found themselves put to work in a range of tasks. It is fair to assume that some, both male and female, were used for sex; indeed, it may have been the very purpose of their seizure. Finally, the commission of crime was a talent that was likely imparted to select captives, especially if their captor made raiding his permanent business.

To sum up, captives can be characterized as slaves who lacked both rights to legal protection and visibility as accepted members of society.

* * *

Combatting abduction and its attendant violence was not a straightforward enterprise. From ancient times onward, the seizure of humans could bestow an aura of heroic valor on the kidnapper. Among the Ottomans as well as their predecessors and neighbors, abduction was a customary way for men to exhibit power, to intimidate, and to establish their reputation. It was the mark of the victor. But abduction could also become a common local phenomenon, prompted by necessity in times of extreme poverty, for example.

A further obstacle in persuading subjects of the empire that abduction was a criminal act was the fact that the kidnapping of females was a familiar route to marriage, especially in rural areas. "Marital abduction" was a way around a male relative's disapproval of matches made for his female relatives, as a case from the eastern Anatolian province of Harput in the mid-seventeenth century demonstrates. Ebu Bekir refuses to give his sister Güllü in marriage to his paternal cousin Osman, who claims that Ebu Bekir's now-deceased father had promised Güllü to *him*. Rather than go to court, Osman, together with his father and brother plus two others, abducts Güllü. In the process, the men lock up her mother and tie up her brother.[1] Güllü's own thoughts are nowhere revealed, although her silence suggests she may not be unhappy with the outcome.

The fact that females could be complicit in their kidnapping added to the frequency of abduction and might lend it an aura of adventure. Poverty, a different factor, could make it difficult for young men to find brides, hence the utility of elopement or the riskier option of abducting a female who was not complicit. The line between "civilian" and "outlaw" abduction could therefore be hazy. For this reason, the black-market sale of women was no doubt a boon for many. Unfortunately, such markets are virtually invisible in the historical record.

From antiquity onward, captive-taking had a persistent presence in Anatolia. Various Hittite statutes from the fifteenth to the thirteenth centuries BC bear a strikingly similar syntax to those of sixteenth-century Ottoman law: for example, "If anyone breaks a male or female slave's arm or leg, he shall pay ten shekels of silver."[2] A millennium later, a Roman digest on the duties of a provincial governor prescribed that "he must hunt down desecrators and pillagers of sacred property, bandits, kidnappers, and common thieves and punish each one in accordance with his misdeeds."[3] When, in 51 BC, the Roman orator and statesman Cicero took up his governorship of Cilicia (the southern Mediterranean coast of Anatolia), things had not much improved. The same could fairly be said of the Ottoman sixteenth century, when it was an inescapable reality that raiding often served as a principal economic resource for some tribal groups and an alternative livelihood for settled communities in hard times.

As a consequence of these cultural and economic habits, state authorities faced an uphill battle in their efforts to persuade some sectors of the population that abduction was a criminal act and the abductor an outlaw. It was not until the late fifteenth century that Ottoman sultans formally acknowledged abduction as a crime: Bayezid II (r. 1481–1512) introduced it in the *Kanunname-i Osmanî* (Ottoman Statute Book), originated some twenty years earlier by his father Mehmed the Conqueror. Kanunname statutes pertaining to sexual crime were adapted from Islamic law, and prescribed punishments were based on *ta'zir,* the canonical imposition of flogging and/or fines at the judge's discretion.

Bayezid confirmed these rules, but more importantly, he introduced an extensive new section to the Kanunname that addressed common crimes whose punishments were largely derived from customary law.[4] It is here, in the lengthy opening statute, that the penalty of castration was prescribed for the crime of abducting a girl or boy. A linked statute pronounced that an abductor who forcibly imposed marriage on a girl or woman was to be divorced from her, while the cleric who performed the marriage suffered severe beating and the humiliation of having his beard cut off. It is not clear that these penalties were widely applied; nevertheless, the threat of invoking them was ever present, as the petitions below demonstrate.

The Kanunname was a fluid body of statutes that successive sultans amended with new or revised rules. Introduced between 1541 and 1545, Suleyman's updated edition worked to further align imperial law with crime on the ground. Regarding abduction, his principal contribution was two new statutes that addressed female accountability in sexual crime. Women and girls were now compelled to pay the same fine as males for fornication or adultery (until then the responsibility of the father or the cuckolded husband). As for abduction, females who consented to their capture were now to have their genitals branded, a punishment perhaps regarded as a female analog to castration. (This may have been a rarely applied penalty.)[5] Expanding culpability further, Suleyman's Kanunname also imposed castration on accomplices to an abduction. (Castration was also being applied in Europe: it became a capital crime in England in 1535, while Florence had already passed statutes in 1325 punishing the sodomite with castration, harsh fines, and other corporal penalties.)[6]

To be sure, bolstering the law did not mean the erasure of abduction, but at least it reinforced the state's sanction to prosecute it. The reach of the law was expanding under Suleyman: like women, now slaves and non-Muslims were made liable for half the fines imposed on Muslim males. What we might call "the legal nation" thus came to include all subjects of the sultanate. (The only exception was the large body of kul, who were punished within the imperial household they served.)

In a different development of Suleyman's reign, the royal chancery (which drafted Kanunname reissues) began in the 1550s to systematically archive its official communications with the increasingly numerous

45

Ottoman provinces. Reports of criminal activity and the sultanate's responses were recorded alongside myriad other matters of state and collected in compendia known as Registers of Important Affairs (*Mühimme Defterleri*). Complaints regarding criminal abduction took the form of petitions from communities suffering from captive-taking and its attendant violence. The Mühimme registers detailed imperial responses that typically instructed local authorities to pursue and punish culprits; in egregious cases, the perpetrators were to be sent to Istanbul to be further tried. While such orders were issued in the sultan's voice, they were generally the outcome of deliberations in the Imperial Council, with the sultan or grand vezir present for the most critical issues. The Council comprised the sultan's top statesmen, among them the chancellor, whose bailiwick included the Kanunname.

The right of subjects to petition the sovereign was a venerable tradition in the Muslim Middle East. A noteworthy significance of the Mühimme registers is their preservation of a wide spectrum of dialogue between provincial petitioners and imperial authorities.

* * *

Four samples of petitions reporting crimes against individuals will serve as an introduction to the communications between the sultanate and provincial authorities. The petitions appear in the third of the Mühimme registers. More comprehensive than its predecessors, it covered the two-year period between December 1558 and December 1560, and can be considered a step forward in imperial record-keeping. Petitions dealing with abduction typically represented a last, often desperate, appeal for aid that followed the failure or incapacity of local resources to free captives and punish their captors. In addition to local posses, these resources included various Ottoman officials assigned to provincial capitals—police superintendents, governors, judges, and locally-stationed timariot soldiers.[7] As for the accused, they ranged from practiced and notorious brigands and highwaymen to local rowdies who crossed the line into what was now classified as criminal activity. The extensive lexicon of labels applied to abductors, both official and vernacular, is no surprise.

Abduction was typically a domestic phenomenon, often coupled with the crime of breaking down the door of a dwelling and "entering with malicious intent." Such house raiding (*ev basma*) could also be compounded by theft, destruction of property, and/or murder. Here too, Bayezid II was the first to criminalize this act of multiple violence, once again imposing castration on the perpetrator. House raiding had historically been a heavily punished offence among Eurasian polities that preceded the Ottomans. Notably, it had been severely criminalized by the Turkmen principality of Dulkadir, annexed by the Ottomans in 1521. Both Selim and Suleyman, and probably Bayezid before them, were influenced by the Dulkadir Kanunname.[8] It was also studied by chancery officials.

Our first petition comes from the town of Göynük, located in northwestern Anatolia. It recounted "matters of the utmost urgency," namely, abductions perpetrated by four individuals.[9] The first, a local "freebooter," was accused by a villager of abducting and holding his wife for a week, inflicting "many outrages" on her; this allegation was followed by "a multitude" of individuals who testified that the abductor was also "a thief and a bandit." The petition next named two madrasa students, brothers from a tribal village, who had abducted "girls and boys." This unfortunate habit among some madrasa students appears to have stemmed from their sense of entitlement to human chattel (madrasas were selective). It was a measure of the challenge in persuading society that privileged status was a license neither to acquire human property nor to disregard the law.

The last of the four outlaws was another freebooter who was accused of "stealing" an unnamed man. (The verb "steal," often used in the seizure of adult males, underlines the loss to both the community and his family when a household head vanishes.) The petition emphasized that the "seditious conduct" of the captor "has no end" and that he disappeared at the time of investigation. The sultan's response, addressed to the local judge, urged him to make every effort to apprehend the criminals and transport them to Istanbul.

From Lovcha in northern Bulgaria came a petition that dramatized the raw fear suffered by local populations.[10] In typical formulaic vocabulary, it cited the "multitude" of villains who "do not obey the laws of Allah or those of the Sultan," who are "given to depravity and debauchery," and who seize girls and boys and steal men. The petition then went on to recount an alarming incident that had taken place during an unrelated hearing in one of the district's villages (the issue was "the circumstances of the poor"). Storming the hearing, the drunken son of a local timariot created panic by repeatedly brandishing his sword and then stabbing bystanders with his dagger. Shouts to "catch him!" were answered with fear of reprisal: "he'll cut us to pieces," "we won't be able to get to our fields," "he'll set fire to our houses."

Such was the license presumed by this son of a local military functionary, a delegate of government authority. Unfortunately, there were other timariots who considered themselves untouchable as members of a privileged class. In the case of Lovcha, at least channels of communication between the suffering villagers and the sultanate proved effective. The imperial response called for the capture of the rioter and his accomplice "by whatever means, but with caution." Capture was to be followed by indictment and then, if the accused were found guilty, deportation in chains to the imperial capital for further trial and punishment.

This next case, from south-central Anatolia, may suggest that criminal behavior was not always locally generated and that imperial politics might touch off local crime, directly or indirectly.[11] Several individuals—Divane ("Mad") Mustafa, Koca, Aydın, "and others"—were "ceaselessly" abducting the sons and male slaves of "good families"; in addition, they forcibly seized women and, in general, perpetrated all manner of "sedition and abomination." (This phrase was a classic ritual condemnation of foul and brutal acts.) Some eight months earlier, however, the accused had been employed as soldiers serving Suleyman's son Bayezid in the Battle of Konya, a showdown between the prince and his older brother Selim. The latter emerged victorious, and Bayezid disappeared, fleeing to Iran to escape his father's wrath.

As for the demobilized soldiers, we might imagine that their criminal turn resulted from difficulty in finding steady employment, especially as they had lost their patron. On the other hand, perhaps they were motivated to disturb the peace of the realm out of resentment toward the sultan, who had openly backed Selim and was now persecuting the prince they had served. Bayezid had garnered admiration and sympathy among significant factions of the army and the empire's populace, while Selim was widely disliked among both the civilian and the military populations.

Exacerbating the threat of violent assault was the fact that perpetrators of crime sometimes found local collaborators, among them provincial appointees of the sultanate. A prime example of this double menace was the case of corrupt judges who were conniving with "gangs of nomads."[12] The latter were accused of "killing people on the roads," presumably while or after robbing them. The petition went on to describe the nomads as "people of abomination," suggesting that they were kidnappers and possibly rapists as well as murderers. As for the judges, their crime was taking bribes from the accused by "accepting some of their gold" in exchange for feigning trials that let them go free.

The prosecution of both parties was assigned to one Mevlana Emirshah, former judge of Ankara and presumably an experienced and trusted individual. The double breach of the law apparently warranted reinforcement: Suleyman dispatched a royal envoy (çavuş) to serve as court sergeant. Danger on the roads was a perennial fear, as it threatened not only local populations but also travelers, long-distance traders, pilgrims, and state officials posted to various provinces. The four afflicted districts were located in highland regions along the vital route between Ankara and Istanbul.

Highway robbery, a scenario that often included abduction, was one of the five capital crimes in Islamic law. It was the first crime cited in the Dulkadir lawbook—the punishment was hanging by the neck and severe torture.[13] The Ottoman lawbook did not formally include it, presumably because prosecution and sentencing of this crime rested in the hands not of a judge but rather of the ruler (who stood in lieu of God). Orders from the Imperial Council to Mevlana Emirshah prescribed the most violent forms of death by execution: dismemberment or a choice among hanging, impalement, and crucifixion. The punishment was to be carried out in the criminal's home territory as a deterrent to heinous crime. Those whose participation in the crime did not merit the death sentence were to be sent to the capital in chains. As for the judges, their unholy alliance with the nomad gangs and their sham trials were presumably punished by the empire's chief mufti, who headed the large corporation of bureaucrats trained in religious sciences and the law.

If the governor Cicero had confronted similar malfeasance in Cilicia, he would not have been unduly surprised at the collaboration between the bandits and the judges. Roman law took for granted that brigands could not manage without co-conspirators ("without them the bandit cannot long remain hidden").[14]

* * *

This last case raises the critical question of how tightly the imperial regime was able to control its provincial territories and the delegates of its authority. It is typically assumed that the empire was generally well managed by the mid-sixteenth century, thanks in part to the longevity and relative order of Suleyman's reign (1520–1566). He was the last of the four sultans who consolidated imperial rule and imperial law in an intense era that had begun with the conquest of Constantinople in 1453.

This does not mean that the provinces were evenly monitored or that they sent petitions to Istanbul at similar rates. It was true that in 1558 the Imperial Council was dispatching administrative orders to the farthest outposts of the empire—Buda (today, in Hungary), Van (in eastern/southeastern Anatolia), and Basra (today in Iraq), for example. However, its numerous responses to reports of local brigandage, including abduction, were largely confined to the "core" Anatolian regions assimilated during the fourteenth and fifteenth centuries: the northwest, the central region from the Black Sea to the Mediterranean Sea, and the smaller northeast region up to and including Trabzon. Southeastern Anatolia, absorbed by Selim I forty years earlier in a prelude to his conquest of the Mamluk empire, was apparently not yet part of the Anatolian "social safety network," so to speak. This was despite the robust incidence of raiding and kidnappings in this quasi-tribal region. The core empire, it seems, was what it had been at the end of Mehmed the Conqueror's reign.

Initial inattention to southeastern Anatolia appears to have been a problem primarily of underdeveloped communications and contact. The process of integrating these new territories into a still-expanding imperial entity could lag. Among the factors that slowed assimilation were the region's lack of major cities (such as the large urban capitals of Aleppo, Damascus, and Cairo to the south), Selim's unexpected death in 1520, and Suleyman's ten military campaigns, some lasting nearly two years. A different kind of contributing factor was the relatively small cadre of scribal bureaucrats working in the imperial chancery and treasury offices (their ranks would expand in the later sixteenth century).

Aintab, a province in southeastern Anatolia, serves usefully for a micro-study of one territory's gradual incorporation into imperial systems of government and the linked efforts to forestall crime. It was at this local level that criminal enterprise was most effectively understood and confronted. By looking simultaneously at imperial initiatives at the provincial level and the strategies of local actors, we gain a more nuanced understanding of on-the-ground endeavors to deter violence. Looking locally can also open windows onto both the challenges and the strategies that characterized the assimilation of distant domains.

Aintab was a relatively small province whose capital city served as a strategic bastion due to its recently refurbished citadel. During the summer of 1516, Selim spent several days in Aintab and its environs, preparing for his first confrontation with the Mamluk army. During that time, the sultan and the city elders negotiated the province's surrender to the Ottomans, which was apparently cordial. The ensuing integration of Aintab into state mechanisms of administration would prove to be a stop-and-start process, although a relationship of mutual accommodation would be evident by the 1550s in what we might call a process of managerial consolidation. Initially, a rudimentary command structure—state-appointed police superintendent and military governor—was put in place, followed by the assignment of timariot soldiers to duty in villages. Taxes were imposed and local agents were commissioned to collect the state's share.

In this early period, Aintab relied more closely on regional than imperial networks and practices. The province was first assigned to the Ottoman governorate-general of Aleppo, then later shifted to that of Dulkadir to the north, where it would remain.[15] The two governorates possessed quite different cultures and political histories, the one an ancient Arab urban capital, the other a tenacious Turkmen frontier state. Istanbul's decision to transfer Aintab to Dulkadir was likely connected, in part at least, to the continuing threat from the east of Safavid Iran's ideological and military infiltration.

It was only in 1536, on the heels of Suleyman's first victory over Iran, that the sultanate focused on the need to subject southeastern provinces to greater oversight from Istanbul. In that year, Aintab was assigned its first *tahrir*, a state-managed inventory comprising population census and survey of productive lands as well as urban enterprises. A second, more thorough tahrir would follow in 1543 that would provide opportunity to address public order. It would also enable the sultanate to benefit from Aintab's growing prosperity (thus rising tax revenue) as the region recovered from the destructive contest for control that preceded

Selim's victories. One effect had been peasant flight from rural areas. Weakening security was an invitation to crime.

* * *

In June 1541, the first state-appointed judge arrived in Aintab, almost certainly bearing Suleyman's latest redaction of the Ottoman Statute Book. This was a watershed moment since court investigations and rulings now carried the force of imperial scrutiny and authority. No time was wasted in demonstrating this reality. Two days before the judge's arrival, a special agent— "the imperial slave Ahmed Beg"—appeared in Aintab on assignment to recover arrears incurred by two local tax-farming notables. The errant tax agents had failed to turn over to Istanbul three years' worth of revenue from crown lands in the province.

The sultanate apparently intended to make an example of these prominent Aintab entrepreneurs. Each had to liquidate property and investments to cover his debts, a procedure presided over publicly by the new judge. The slave girls Selvareh and Harireh in chapter one were among the possessions sold by Ali Sikkakoğlu, the now somewhat disgraced former secretary of the crown lands and head of one of the province's three notable lineages.[16]

The status of land and its tax revenues was a matter to which Suleyman had already been attentive, in part because of its links to the control of crime, abduction included. On his mind were rural lands that earlier sultans had gifted to notables and/or timariot soldiers. Such freehold ownership (*serbestiyet*) carried the right to collect taxes on rural land and its products.[17] As will be seen, freeholders in Aintab played mixed roles in Suleyman's strategies to combat criminal activity.

Sultans had typically awarded freehold grants in moments of military challenge or dynastic weakness, their goal was to gain the backing of supporters. Selim had done the same in Aintab, assigning the revenue of one of the province's villages to a local holy man and his progeny. The recipient's distinction was that his eminent father, Sheikh Abdurrahman Erzincani, had openly broken with the Safavids over religious doctrine. Settling in eastern Anatolia, the sheikh acquired his own disciples and received support from the sultanate. Selim wanted this spiritual lineage firmly anchored on the Ottoman side.[18]

In addition to their spiritual responsibilities, sheikhly freeholders like Erzincani's son might play entrepreneurial roles linked to their fiscal obligations. Sheikhs were not necessarily exemplary citizens. On the day that the special agent arraigned the two tax farmers, he also summoned Sheikh Ismail, head of the prominent Haji Baba religious retreat (a sufi of dervish lodge, or, as they were known in this region, a *zaviye*). He too had been negligent, failing to remit the sultanate's share of revenue from the rich village of Mervane, the preponderance of which constituted the freehold grant that supported the zaviye and provided his salary. Like Ali Sikkakoğlu, Sheikh Ismail was head of a prominent lineage; his son Şemseddin was head of another one of the province's distinguished retreats.[19]

A more troubling aspect of freehold donations was that their recipients had come to assert privileges that interfered with imperial policy, in particular, with the control of abduction. The issue was that freeholders were claiming the right to try and punish criminals apprehended on their properties. In part to address this situation, the second Aintab tahrir inventory in 1543 returned to an older taxation system long familiar in the region. One outcome was the restoration to the sultanate of partial rights to freehold land.

With its access to freehold administration reclaimed, the state could now take steps to curb abuses. An immediate challenge was the fact that freeholders had been denying state-appointed police superintendents' entry to their villages, prompting one historian to label the latter "sanctuaries" for criminals.[20] To make matters worse, these same freeholders claimed for themselves the fines that they had imposed on the guilty. In other words, rural administration could have a decided impact on the state's efforts to prosecute crimes of violence, especially as the majority of kidnappings occurred in villages and their environs. Let us remember that abduction was still regarded among some as proof of valor.

Mühimme Register Three makes amply clear the frustrations arising from imperial efforts to restore state control of criminal prosecution on freehold land. A royal dispatch to the governor of Bursa complained that this large province's villages, predominantly freehold, were overrun with brigands because timariots were insisting that "jailing is our right!" Consequently, "more and more men of abomination" were raiding houses and killing people. The dispatch ordered local state authorities to jail suspects, try them, and execute the worst of the guilty in their home environs.[21] We can safely assume that the house-raiding led to a number of kidnappings.

In Aydın province (in the Aegean region), things were apparently worse.[22] Timariots had incarcerated so many wrongdoers that the latters' "orphan" sons had themselves turned to banditry to cover the debts of their fathers. More alarming, the same criminal acts were being committed by timariots themselves and also by men of other military ranks stationed in the province. Hanging or dismemberment was prescribed as the punishment for such "obscene crimes." Additionally, the sultan was to be informed of any signs of resistance to punishing the guilty or any protests against the stipulated penalties. The tenor of this imperial order was palpably overwrought.

* * *

The sultanate's restored access to freehold administration in Aintab provided a second, quite different, opportunity to challenge local criminal activity. This was Istanbul's ability to influence the practice of charity in favor of state priorities, a phenomenon that has gone largely unrecognized because of its indirect nature. One of these priorities was safety and security on major roads. Rural depopulation stemming from the rivalry among Mamluks, Ottomans, and the Dulkadir for control of the region had rendered thoroughfares less safe and more vulnerable to brigand attacks. By the mid-1540s, however, Aintab's economic recovery was visible in rising intraprovincial commerce as well as greater interregional traffic. In addition to trade routes to the east and northwest established in ancient times, the victories of Selim and Suleyman had reanimated the linked arteries comprising the Fertile Crescent. Aintab was located at the apex of the crescent.

Now the problem was highway bandits eager to exploit the fruits of economic recovery. Ample evidence of their assaults was recorded at the Aintab court in 1541, when the sultanate was in the process of upgrading its attention to the province. In April, testimony was supplied by a man who had been severely wounded in an attack on the caravan he was escorting to Mosul. Despite his dire condition, he managed to tell his story to the judge so that local villagers would not be held responsible for his approaching death.[23] Some months later, when rumors reached Aintab that a resident of the city had murdered a traveling merchant, an influential local citizen went to court to register his threat of a formal "disgracing" of the alleged perpetrator (presumably in addition to the judge's own investigation).[24] Disgracing typically involved exposing an individual to public censure and/or humiliation.

How exactly did freehold tenure figure in the sultanate's ability to influence local philanthropy in the quest for regional security? One strategy was to enhance support for institutions that could contribute, directly or indirectly, to safer movement within the province. Among these institutions were the *zaviyes*. These spiritual retreats were typically supported by local charitable donations from freeholders and/or sultanic philanthropy. A common custom, indeed an expectation, was that freeholders would dedicate some part of their tax revenues to charitable foundations (*waqf*). (Similar endowments had existed in Aintab long before the Muslim conquest of the 660s.) The more substantial foundations attracted not only the benefaction of ruling dynasties but also their scrutiny. The same held true under Muslim monarchs who had exercised control over Aintab, most recently the Mamluk and Dulkadir sovereigns.

The sultanate's initial intervention into foundation management in Aintab was a summons issued in October 1540 ordering the registration of all rural lands supporting charitable waqfs. Over the course of five days, a procession of freeholders appeared before the Aintab judge together with witnesses able to confirm their ownership claims. Mehmed the Conqueror had set a precedent with such an investigation, the outcome of which was partial restoration of the state's share in lands dedicated to waqfs that had fallen into disuse.[25] This was a scenario recently replicated in Aintab.

Then later, when the last of Suleyman's three wars with Iran ended in 1555 and peace treaties were settled with the Safavid shah and the Hapsburg emperor in Vienna, it was an opportune time to step up aspects of imperial governance in Aintab. In 1557, Ottoman authorities ordered another survey of Aintab's charitable foundations. The official register compiled by the survey team assessed fiscal well-being by recording both sources of income and expenditures for three categories of charitable foundations: mosques, madrasas and preparatory schools, and zaviyes. A major purpose of the survey was to certify the degree of recovery of waqf institutions that had fallen into decline. It was clear that the province's spiritual retreats had been the hardest-hit waqfs in the unsettled decades immediately preceding and following the Ottoman conquest. The new register helped to cast light on the ups and downs waqfs had experienced since the demise of the Mamluks. In particular, a major goal of the highly detailed review of zaviye fortunes appears to have been the restoration to full potential of the province's spiritual infrastructure.

Whether intended or not, one outcome of the restitution of zaviyes was greater security for those who travelled on Aintab's roads. (The majority of zaviyes were located in villages or their vicinities.) Economic decline and rural depopulation had weakened their income base, causing some to effectively cease operation. However, at least eight were functioning again by 1557, having profited from economic and commercial recovery and underwritten in part by the sultanate.

The significant contributions of spiritual retreats to both local and imperial well-being have generally been ignored, in particular, the important work they performed in provincial settings. As might be expected, zaviyes offered religious community and the counsel provided by the resident sheikh or baba. If the premises included the tomb of a saintly figure to whom one could offer prayer, all the better. Zaviyes located in or near rural settlements were a boon to Muslim travelers, who could fulfill their religious obligations while on the road.

However, the 1557 survey made clear that spiritual sustenance was not the only or even the principal function of Aintab's zaviyes. A core function of the better-endowed retreats was the provision of soup kitchens that fed both the local poor and travelers. These two populations were cited in the Qur'an as persons deserving of charity.[26] Zaviye soup kitchens typically operated both morning and evening, some providing special meals for religious holidays. In addition to feeding, some zaviyes had the capacity to furnish their visitors with a place to sleep.

The hospitality functions of these institutions meant that investing in them was also investing in the empire's security. In addition to addressing basic needs of travelers, zaviyes provided geographical markers. An example is the Dülük Baba zaviye, 15 kilometers (about 9 miles) north of Aintab city. In 1557, it was by far the largest of three recovering spiritual retreats that had earlier been under Mamluk patronage. This ancient sanctuary had hosted Teshub, the Hittite god of sky and storm, and then later the Roman mystery cult of Jupiter Dolichenus, carried westward by soldiers returning from service in the east.[27] In early medieval times, Dülük had been a larger city than Aintab, but then was destroyed in a fourteenth-century earthquake; it was now a good-sized village. This tenacious survival of the settlement at Dülük testifies to the power of its spiritual pedigree. Its shrine also owed something to its proximity to several intersecting routes traversing the province.

One of the numerous legends about Dülük recounted over the centuries suggests that preventing a retreat from falling into disrepair was a concern on people's minds. As the story went, the holy man's grave fell into obscurity over time, until a mule driver got lost in a storm on his way to Aintab city. When he sought help in prayer from his spiritual guide, the latter miraculously appeared before him, only to observe that he was not needed: a flashing light pointed to Dülük Baba's grave. The tale specifically underlines the utility of spiritual retreats as route markers: the flashing light illuminated the mule driver's road forward. When he later returned to construct a tomb for Dülük Baba, he also established an endowment to keep a lantern lit at night to guide sojourners.[28]

It was not surprising that Selim, the first Ottoman patron of the shrine, entered local lore along with Dülük Baba. In a story told by the seventeenth-century courtier Evliya Çelebi, Dülük Baba is a miracle worker taking the form of a dervish living at the time of the Ottoman conquest. As Sultan Selim marches through the province, the dervish approaches him with the good tidings of the conquest to come, predicting the date on which the Ottoman army would take Cairo. When things turn out as Dülük Baba had anticipated, the victorious sultan returns to Aintab to honor him, only to find that the dervish has passed away. Before departing for Istanbul, Selim builds a lofty tomb over his grave.[29] The reader/listener understands that it is this act of benefaction that gives new life to the shrine and its environs.

* * *

Over time, Aintab and other provinces grew from dependencies of the conquest state into participant components of the Ottoman sultanate. By 1558, the empire was in relatively good working order given that early modern states rarely enjoyed comprehensive oversight of their territories. But if its infrastructure was developing with an eye to administrative and legal cohesion, things were coming loose in other ways. Aintab had experienced notable growth between and beyond the surveys of 1536 and 1543, but a subsequent survey, in 1574, demonstrated stagnation, if not decline.

After more than a century of expansion, the empire was beginning to experience a period of challenge and adjustment that lasted for several decades. Political and military difficulties were compounded by factors beyond the sultanate's control. These included periodic weather crises (effects of the Little Ice Age) and fiscal disruptions that swept eastward across continents. In addition, the very prosperity of the Mediterranean region had a downside: it enabled the Ottoman population to double between roughly 1525 and 1575, eventually creating a problem of pressure on the land. One symptom of declining rural well-being was the rise in the number of bachelors, males who lacked the wherewithal to acquire a bride and establish a household. One tried and true strategy to get a wife in straitened times was to abduct her or visit a black market. Stresses like these were apparently greatest in Anatolia.

What has generally been known as "the crisis of the seventeenth century" manifested itself in the Ottoman zones as early as the 1570s, when a number of disturbing developments began to confront the empire. Inflation followed by currency debasement hurt those on fixed incomes, Janissaries and shopkeepers alike. Military campaigns now rarely won substantial new territories that could be relied on to provide revenues, jobs, and investment opportunities. War was becoming a financial drain and subjects were confronted by new kinds of government-issued taxes to meet budgetary shortfalls.

Meanwhile, a gradual shift in political power was beginning to take place. The dominance of the sultan, as both ruler and commander, was giving way to the rise of vezirs and pashas who vied for influence. Suleyman, who died in 1566, would be the last warrior sultan for nearly a century, and while his occasional successor led troops in battle, decisive victories were becoming rare. There had even been a moment when a foreign ambassador wondered who would succeed to the Ottoman domains if the empire were to collapse. At least this period served to maintain the survival of the Ottomans at a time when other states were yielding to new monarchies (the Rurik to the Romanov in Russia, the Ming to the Ching in China). Elsewhere civil war divided polities, as in England.

It took the Ottomans from the 1570s to the 1640s to complete the transition from warrior to palace sultan. Leading members of the kul—high-ranking military and political figures trained in the vast imperial household—had always been influential, but now their own large households were vital. The gradual sedentarization of the sultanate led to greater reliance on these powerful figures, who were under pressure to recruit greater numbers of combat-ready soldiers. Originally captives themselves, vezirs and pashas now enjoyed a robust sense of entitlement to human booty. On the other hand, it was getting harder to take prisoners in war, as combat frequently ended in stalemate instead of victory. Frontiers were now more distant and captives less accessible, while the flourishing trade in ransoming prisoners consumed a share of human booty. The unfortunate consequence was that free subjects of the sultanate were increasingly regarded as a source of captives.

Toward the end of the sixteenth century, an epidemic of brigandage spread across the Rumelian and Anatolian domains of the empire, continuing in waves well into the seventeenth century. Individuals, bands and gangs, civilians and soldiers, and even imperial officials seized married women, young boys, and young girls (*virgin* girls, as contemporary sources took care to note). In communications circulating between Istanbul and the provinces, a rich vocabulary of defiance and insubordination was leveled against these outlaws: countless accusations employed epithets such as *fomenter of disorder, sedition,* and/or *insurrection; robber; bastard villain; rebel; the cruel* and *the unjust, the tyrannous,* and, most commonly, *brigand.*[30]

The year 1603, when the "long war" with the Austrian Hapsburgs was still carrying on, was a low point. Second-tier officers were pushing their way into command posts through the unsavory tactic of recruiting both soldiers and auxiliaries from discontented groups known as *sekban* (armed civilian mercenaries) and *jelali* (a term encompassing both rebel and bandit). They also attracted Anatolian peasants furloughed from the Austrian war who, having learned the use of firearms, were more interested in new horizons than the family farm.

The historian Ibrahim Peçevi (d. 1650) recounted a story of two *jelali* brothers, the first of whom was killed during his armed campaign across Anatolia in defiance of imperial orders. The other brother, Deli ("Mad") Hasan, fared somewhat better. Raising an army of an alleged 30,000 men, he wreaked havoc across central Anatolia, leading to the death of two pashas sent against him. The solution was apparently to buy him off with the governorship of Bosnia (plus six fiefs for his "brigands") and send him against the Hungarians. In a way, Deli Hasan is reminiscent of the gunslingers of the nineteenth-century American west, some of whom were both outlaw and lawman.

Deli Hasan's misdeeds only escalated, however. "If he obeyed one day, he didn't for [the next] five." Peçevi commented that the many tales accumulating around him were like a snake unfurling itself (one was his offer to sell Ottoman fortresses to Venice, the Pope, and Spain). Hasan's chronic recklessness eventually caught up with him, culminating in a sentence of exile to the Eyalet of Temeşvar (a region referred to as the Banat Region). It is at this point that Peçevi's story takes an unexpected turn, revealing that the crux of his narrative is less the jelali's violent conduct than the observation that people tend to admire a successful bandit. Deli Hasan's guards apparently felt compelled to bypass Belgrade en route to Romania because the city's residents were likely not only to laud a successful bandit but also to shelter him.

This story reminds us that, while our sources rarely mention sympathizers and accomplices, colorful bandits might attract allies, especially at times when state measures of discipline were themselves oppressive—or, as in this case, futile. Moreover, bandits and brigands, like cowboys, might engage in a form of "redistribution of wealth" from which local populations might benefit. Communities suffering from insufficient means might themselves be compelled to take up raiding, another stimulus for tolerance of the "outlaw."

Rogue contingents were not always made up of military. "Civilian" brigands engaged in menacing exploits as well, both on their own or in league with figures like Deli Hasan. One of the most egregious events of this "age of brigands" occurred when in 1637 the sultan Murat IV announced a military campaign to recover Baghdad, which had been recently conquered by the Safavids. Soldiers summoned for duty, however, had other kinds of gain in mind that apparently included collaboration with local brigands. The danger was spelled out in the sultan's bulletin of alarm, which was dispatched to judges stationed in cities and towns along three of the empire's main arteries, where they served as communication and nerve centers:

At present, most of my Janissaries who are stationed in the capitals of your judicial districts do not muster for my imperial campaign. And some of them go to Akkirman province to engage in trade and purchase slaves. They are of one heart and one mind with brigands, and some of them enter the homes of the people and attempt to take their wives and sons, and they seize many girls with the intention of raping them, and they set fire to the houses [of the people], and they murder people. Moreover, they do not muster for my imperial campaign. In particular, [when] the community of Muhammad are united in their labor in the trenches of Baghdad, City of Peace, sacrificing body and soul, these individuals pursue only their own profit and gain and seek only [the satisfaction of] lust and luxury. (Mühimme Register 85, Order #103 [7 January 1631], 64–65)

The only warrior sultan of the long transition period, Murad did succeed in regaining Baghdad from the Safavids as he had Yerevan three years earlier. He named the two beautiful victory pavilions that he ordered for the Topkapı Palace after these recovered capitals of Iraq and Armenia.

Murad's bulletin to the judges is recorded in a Mühimme Register (No. 85). In comparison to the registers of Suleyman's time, the criminal acts now being addressed were larger in scale and more consequential in their damages. If Mühimmes were an index of where state resources most needed to be marshalled, then it may be that local brigandage was receiving less attention than it had a century earlier. The escalation of criminal defiance demonstrated by Murad's soldiers was due in part to the fact that the empire was no longer on a regular war footing and thus unable to support its troops. The security of Anatolia appears to have taken second place to the defense of two critical frontiers, with Hungary and Iran.

Given that instances of crime committed by solo brigands were likely becoming less commonly reported, it may have taken a particularly influential plaintiff or a dastardly perpetrator to bring as serious a case to Istanbul's attention. In 1630, when an Anatolian judge, Mevlana Mustafa, called in a loan of 50,000 silver coins (akçe) from a certain Hüseyin, the latter used it as a pretext to carry off the judge's wife Emine. Hüseyin was alleged to have handed her over to one of his followers "to use." In a rare admission of collective frustration and perhaps embarrassment, the petition of complaint submitted to the Imperial Council noted that "not one of the leading men of the province was capable of rescuing her."[31] This appeal to the sultanate underlined the damage such acts of violence created, not only to personal honor, but also to the collective honor of the local community and, by implication, to the state, which was now charged with the responsibility for the unfortunate woman's salvation.

This case raises the question of when a person has crossed the line into criminal banditry. Was Hüseyin, who was labeled in the petition a "brigand captain" of a gang of forty-some men, a recognized outlaw or a victim of the increasingly hyper accusatory rhetoric typical of the times?[32] He appears to have had legitimate relations with a judge of some stature. The size of the loan, no minor transaction, gives pause, suggesting that a degree of trust had existed between the two men. Hüseyin had clearly perpetrated a serious crime, but that didn't mean that he was a "career" bandit. We might imagine him as an entrepreneur with numerous dependents—a prominent individual with a following—rather than a predator holed up with his gang. (Recall that individuals of note had entourages.) If so, the case may suggest that abduction was not a resource confined to the desperate or the confirmed criminal. It also raises the question of just how commonly abduction was intended as an act of reprisal.

If plunder was an entitlement, even Hüseyin's seizure of the judge's wife Emine might conceivably be construed as a plausible reaction to support denied. This is not to say he felt justified in his response to the judge's recall of the loan, but rather that abduction was the most commonly understood response to the denial of expectation.

Chapter Three

Voices of Captivity in Legend, History, and Law

By the reign of Mehmed II, the Conqueror, the Ottoman empire spanned much of the ancient world. The sultans were heir to its culture of conquest as well as its political practices. Enshrined across the region were legends of war and victory, with their stories of heroic battles and trains of war prisoners marched into captivity. Such stories validated both the heroism and the strategic planning that underlay the seizure of enemy soldiers, commoners, and sometimes royalty. The supreme model of the military leader was Alexander the Great, the Macedonian prince who in 331 BC put an end to the great empire of the Persians, thereby joining the Greek world to the Asian. Many of his captives were given to his commanders and Macedonian warriors.

Alexander was a revered figure to the Ottomans. He was celebrated in the earliest illustrated history produced in their domains—the *Iskendername* (Book of Alexander), presented in 1395 to a son of the fourth sultan, Bayezid I.[1] It is likely that Suleyman I had this text read to him;[2] perhaps it was even lodged in his private library. This work and other narratives of the past could inspire, instruct, and caution contemporaries. However, if Suleyman was inspired by Alexander's history, Bayezid's progeny might feel remorseful. The unfortunate sultan had been captured together with his Serbian princess wife by the Turko-Mongol conqueror Timur (Tamerlane). Similarly to his Ottoman counterparts, Timur was heir to a significant measure of Alexander's empire.

Adding insult to injury, Timur was said to have humiliated both Bayezid and his wife. He locked the sultan in an iron cage like a snared animal, while the princess was forced to perform menial service. The magnitude of Bayezid's defeat summoned narrative tropes of extreme humiliation. The story of the two monarchs was retold in opera and works of European literature devoted to their fateful confrontation.

Proving one's enemy incapable of protecting his family was a popular metaphor for preserving the integrity of one's domain. In 1554, when Suleyman was fighting his third campaign against the Safavids of Iran, his wife Hurrem anxiously sent a letter from Istanbul urging him to send news that would placate the local populace. ". . . Neither the son of the heretic nor his wife has been captured," she wrote, "nothing has been happening. Now, if a messenger arrives saying 'no progress here, nothing there', no one is going to be happy, my sultan. . . ."[3] As everyone understood, to abduct the enemy's dependents—often with the unstated presumption of using them for sex—was to level the greatest assault on his honor. In a stunning defeat of the Safavids in 1514, Suleyman's father Selim had set precedent by capturing the previous shah's wife and further humiliating him by turning her over to one of his statesmen.

This preoccupation with abduction and political conflict was not particularly Ottoman. Herodotus had opened his *Histories* with a linked set of abductions that culminated in the conflict over Helen of Troy. Legends of Zeus, king of the gods in Greek mythology, told of the women he abducted and/or raped. Likewise was his practice of capturing youths, most famously Ganymede, whom Homer called "the loveliest of the race of mortals." This prodigious abductor spawned new races with the women he captured, Europa perhaps the best known. Ancient lore noted the creative power that came from such unions of captor and captive. As for the Ottomans, they had ceased making marital alliances with foreign princesses in the early fifteenth century, finding it more profitable at this stage in their development to reproduce the dynasty with select females taken by force from foreign lands.

It was clearly a matter of royal pride to fend off predators who aimed to seize members of one's family. The salience of kidnapped women in the regional discourse of sovereign power was underlined in a late fifteenth-century history of the Akkoyunlu confederation, a rival Anatolian power. To validate the dynasty's claim to "distinguished origin," a celebratory history listed six points, the second of which was that "the hand of a conqueror never touched their spouses."[4] If the Ottomans had to live with the insult to Bayezid I's wife, at least the story was not overtly sexualized.

* * *

Toward the end of the sixteenth century, the numbers of captives taken by the Ottomans in foreign wars were declining. Meanwhile, the empire's own subjects were increasingly falling victim to seizure within its domains. Islamic legal tradition had approved the former with some restrictions, but it was apparently an uphill battle to protect Ottoman subjects.

Enthusiasm for wartime captive-taking had been stimulated in the Ottomans' early decades by popular legends celebrating the successes of Osman, the first in the line of Ottoman sovereigns. These stories inspired some listeners to volunteer for combat and others to become partisans of this rising lineage (Osman's father Ertuğrul, who led Turkic tribes into Anatolia, had himself enjoyed a lauded career). Acknowledged as the first sovereign of the Ottoman dynasty, Osman made his mark as both warlord and political consolidator. His exploits against local magnates, Christian and Muslim alike, quickly became oral legend. Stories of Osman's victories were often narrated by professional storytellers to circles of ardent listeners. Such tales were later included in histories of the early Ottomans that began to circulate toward the later fifteenth century.

One of the most popular of these—Derviş Ahmed Aşıkpaşazade's *Annals of the House of Osman*—drew on both legend and historical research. A major feature of his work was its representation of the frontiersman's perspective and the values that persisted despite the eventual loss of influence by this group. Aşıkpaşazade presents the Ottomans as legitimate claimants to the region east of Bursa, Ertuğrul having been granted authority over it by the Anatolian Seljuk sultan. Discord is the fault of local Byzantine lords, most of whom have been living amicably with these seminomadic Turkish tribes. Tension breaks out, opening the door to Osman's first victory.

This turning point in Aşıkpaşazade's narrative is Osman's *huruç*—his "sallying forth," that is, the emergence of the Ottomans onto the stage of history. Osman must show himself to be a legitimate conqueror, not a usurper. This requires spiritual support, which comes to him in the form of a dream he experiences while praying for worthiness. Unable to comprehend its meaning, he approaches a revered sheikh who interprets it as a sign that he, Osman, has been granted divine sovereignty. Here the narrative breaks into verse, as the sheikh, Edebali, proclaims:

> My son, victory and opportunity are yours, divine guidance and blessings are yours, good fortune is yours.
> May your throne never collapse, for all time past and future fortune is yours.

After some prompting by Edebali's adepts that the unsophisticated warrior should demonstrate his gratitude, Osman gifts the sheikh and his disciples with the sword of his ancestors. The new ruler pledges that his successors will make a pilgrimage to honor the sword and its new spiritual community. In other words, the symbiosis of faith and power will fuel the Ottoman enterprise. Sheikh Edebali's

82

bestowal of his daughter in marriage to Osman further endorses the new lord's stature and his cause.

Aşıkpaşazade's work was completed around 1484, toward the end of his life. At the time, others were also writing histories setting forth the rise and flourishing of the Ottomans. These authors were members of a learned class that had emerged over the previous decades. An intellectual infrastructure had developed among the Ottomans, creating a milieu that nurtured legal scholars, poets, learned mystics, as well as students of the Ottoman past. This maturation had followed a long and painful drive to reassemble the Ottoman polity following its fracturing in the civil war that followed the disastrous fall of Bayezid I. Stability was gradually restored by his grandson Murad II, enabling the flourishing of Ottoman culture that encouraged Aşıkpaşazade and his colleagues. The great mosque complex of Murad's son Mehmed the Conqueror, completed by 1470 in the new capital of Istanbul, was a symbol of the empire's devotion to learning. Its eight madrasas produced scholars, some of whom would carry their learning to provincial centers. Though Aşıkpaşazade grew up in stressful times, he was writing in an era of intellectual expansion.

With a plethora of legends to draw on, writers of the Ottoman past could fashion variant narratives as they valorized the young ruler. A late fifteenth-century account by Mehmed Neşri cast the "emergence" of Osman as the outcome of an abduction. As the story goes, Osman orders his followers to kidnap a young village woman who has resisted his offer of marriage.[5] He had been smitten by the sight of the woman as he passed through the village of Dog's Nose. (Osman had been on his way north to a meeting with the governor of Eski Hisar, a story element suggesting he was now a person of political consequence.) Osman appeals to his father Ertuğrul to intercede with the woman on his behalf, but she demurs, citing the great gap in their social status. The real reason for her resistance, however, was her suspicion that Osman only intended a dalliance that might be the ruination of her reputation. When Osman relates the story to the governor, recounting the woman's excellent attributes, the latter pledges to help him, while secretly planning to seize her for himself. The plot thickens, culminating in a virtual battle among warring factions during which Osman orders his men to abduct Mal Hatun. She is named at this end point in the story, presumably because she now belongs to Osman's household.

Neşri's theme of attraction vs. rejection was taken up and elegantly elaborated by the polymath Kemalpaşhazade Şemseddin Ahmed (1468/69–1534), better known as Ibn Kemal—historian, philosopher, legal scholar and teacher, and, at the end of his career, chief mufti of the empire. Recounted in his chronicle of the dynasty, the abduction story begins as a romance, a spring-time affair of the heart.[6] It is also a "buddy" tale, as Osman is (again) smitten while out hunting with his friends, and it is during a convivial drinking party that he boasts of the woman's beauty—foolishly, as it turns out, for an erstwhile ally secretly connives to take her for himself. It is the revelation of this betrayal that provokes her capture, as in Mehmed Neşri's story. Both tales suggest that the complexities entailed in an abduction, particularly a challenging one, can be a motor for state-building. What ensues in Ibn Kemal's narrative is an armed combat that engages several local lords and provides Osman with his first military victory.

Ibn Kemal's story has a second chapter. If the abduction wins Osman an enhanced reputation as a leader gifted with strategic acuity and military dexterity, the sequel demonstrates how those traits could attract new followers to the Ottoman enterprise. The abduction victory is followed by the conversion of Köse Mihal (Michael, the Beardless), a local Byzantine lord captured in the fray, to both the cause of Osman and to Islam (the two being henceforth inseparable). By the turn of the fifteenth century, when the "House of Mihal" had long since become one of the great warrior lineages fighting alongside the sultans, the story of Mihal's conversion had come to signal the validity in the eyes of God and man of the Ottoman imperial enterprise and to hint at the inevitable collapse of the Byzantine empire.

Overlooked in these celebrations of Osman's first victories are the young women who involuntarily precipitate his rise to power. This is true especially in the case of Ibn Kemal, whose story resembles an eclogue rather than a contest for political dominance. More important, Osman's interest in a particular woman—one who will possibly raise his successor—is ignored. Neşri's story is more "historical": his nod to the young woman's moral rigor suggests he may have had in mind an actual wife of Osman named Mal Hatun. In the end though, she still suffers the indignity of abduction. As with Neşri's story, it is noteworthy that she is named only later in the narrative, by which time the author has recuperated her with a distinguished family pedigree.

To sum up, the narrative logic of Neşri and Ibn Kemal's stories is that abduction affairs are the engine that launches Osman's political career and thus the imperial venture. They are the first and precipitating events that create Osman's path to power. It does not seem to matter that he defies the authority of his father Ertuğrul—both his parental authority (the offers of marriage made without the father's original spon-

sorship or even his awareness) and his political authority (the abduction precipitates factionalism among the
allies of Ertuğrul). Rather, the abductions and their
aftermath appear to signal a new stage for this new
imperial lineage, demonstrating that the young Osman has the desire, the daring, and the leadership
skills to move the small principality onto the stage of
history.

Not all historians of the late fifteenth and early sixteenth centuries feature abduction tales in their
"Histories of the House of Osman." But it is noteworthy that Ibn Kemal's multivolume work was commissioned by the sultan Bayezid II, who reigned from
1481 to 1512, by which time the Ottomans had created an empire. Perhaps the spate of Ottoman annals
during these years was in part an answer to Timur's
humiliation of the early state. Hurrem's worried letter to Suleyman demonstrates the enduring belief that
victory in battle demanded abduction of the enemy's
dependents.

* * *

By the reign of Bayezid II, neither campfire recita-
tions nor historians' tomes were necessary to encour-
age enthusiasm among war volunteers. The principal incentive for civilians who joined up for military

campaigns, mostly on the European frontiers, was the promise of captive bodies and other spoils of victory. Neither supported by the state nor taxed by it, these mounted raiders reaped reward in the form of prisoners who could be sold on open markets or kept for one's own use. Largely summer volunteers, they were typically organized under the leadership of one of the premier military families. But the utility of volunteer raiders was waning by the reign of Mehmed the Conqueror, under whose command both combat and the distribution of its spoils were increasingly centralized. In 1484, however, in preparation for his major campaign into the western Black Sea region, Mehmed's son Bayezid issued a call to arms that promised extravagant rewards to volunteers. Among his pledges were "satiety in booty and . . . riches in plunder."[7]

This was a moment when fiction and reality overlapped. As if drawing on Bayezid's rally, Aşıkpaşazade included in his work of the same years a chapter on Osman's largesse toward volunteers. It told the story of the young new leader's initial military foray, a victory over a local garrison that had turned belligerent. The account concluded, "They took no prisoners. They took a great deal of goods and booty. That is why their following among the people grew." The text then breaks into one of its occasional verses:

They heard about Osman and his ghazis,[8]
That some had got gold and silver, some horses,
That others had got a maiden whom they admired.
At the moment, opportunity lay with the ghazis.
Legions of ghazis rushed to join Osman,
So that his generosity and benefaction
Might continually increase.

Raids were a natural mode of combat for the nascent Ottoman power. The school for raiding was the hunt—later a royal pastime, but in Osman's day a necessity. Other histories of early battles, particularly those of major consequence, lauded the combat strategies of both Osman and his top lieutenants. Raiding had a long history in the Middle East. The term *ghazi* is derived from the Arabic *ghazw,* a raid for purposes of conquest and plunder. Although one fifth of the take belonged to the leader by law, Sultan Bayezid advertised in his call to arms that he would forgo this entitlement during his Black Sea campaign.

The greatest of all military campaigns—the conquest of Constantinople in 1453—drew a range of perspectives on the victory. An early one, that of the historian Mehmed Oruç (Oruç Bey), was yet another text in the celebratory genre of conquest histories. After a siege of fifty-five days, massive ransacking followed the fall of the Byzantine city on May 29th. As

Oruç related it, Sultan Mehmed gave the victorious troops lavish though controlled permission to plunder.

Writing some fifty years after the event, Oruç graphically depicted frenzied scenes of licensed looting:

> [Soldiers] advanced from all sides, deploying force and violence. Making their way into the interior of the fortress, they were relentless in their sack of the city. They seized [the infidels'] sons and daughters and wives and their goods. They plundered whatever they could find by way of gold, silver, pearls, jewels and gold leaf, gold florins, silver aspers, and merchandise. . . . They took anyone they caught in the [infidels'] houses as they were plundering. In this way the warriors for Islam were more than satiated with plunder. They got rich with the riches of war. (Oruç, *Oruç Beg Tarihi*, 78 ff.)

It may well be that the sultan was pained to endorse this inexorable reward. For one thing, the capture and enslavement of young people could deprive the recovering city of a sorely needed resident population of workers and taxpayers. (Mehmed would famously face challenges in repopulating Istanbul.) Such, however, was the unwritten constitution of the empire: combat forces expected to become rich in goods and human capital.

The victorious sultan would mourn other aspects of his victory. Tursun Beg, a timariot who had participated in the siege and who would go on to serve as secretary to Mehmed's governing council, recorded the twenty-one-year-old sultan's reactions. Observing that the outer buildings of the great basilica of Hagia Sophia had fallen into decay in the empire's twilight years, Mehmed "thought of the impermanence and instability of this world, and of its ultimate destruction."

Tursun Beg's was a voice apart from the celebratory writings of his fellow historians. His career as a fighter, particularly at the siege of the new imperial capital, no doubt gave him a different perspective on the magnitude of the victory. The legacy of thirteen centuries of Roman and Byzantine rule was an enormous one to carry.

* * *

A century after his great-grandfather's triumph, Suleyman, himself a distinguished conqueror, faced the limits of empire in his last major battle. His final military confrontation with the Safavid shah of Iran, begun in 1553, ended in drawn-out negotiations and a peace treaty signed two years later. This was not necessarily a bad thing. War was expensive and victory was no longer certain. Combat in distant domains no longer guaranteed new territories or abundant booty, while it could unsettle regions subjected to combat.

History writing too had been shifting since the days of Aşıkpaşazade and Ibn Kemal, from celebratory narratives to nuanced and sometimes critical accounts. New trends and influences such as policy disagreements, a greater range of historical actors, and shifting international alignments influenced histories, as did global factors such as fiscal instability and climate disasters. The historian and provincial official Ibrahim Peçevi was only one of many critical voices as intellectuals and government servants became active in writing essays and submitting memorials to the imperial palace. Peçevi's unusual history drew on his own observations as well as information gleaned from other participant-observers, among them soldiers, commanders, and politicians.

Born in 1574 to a military family in Pécs (Hungary), Peçevi was concerned about laxity on the European frontier, especially as it facilitated the illicit taking of captives (as opposed to prisoners of war). By the late sixteenth century, the sultans had largely withdrawn from the battlefield, with pashas now delegated to take charge. One downside of this shift was the latters' frequent rivalries and clashing opinions over strategy. Factionalism increased and competing pashas often worked at cross purposes. In particular, Peçevi was disturbed by the situation on Hungary's eastern border. He was at the time the treasurer of the kingdom's Danube region.

One matter of concern was that the masses of troops recently deployed in Wallachia had been agitating to take up arms in Hungary. Booty-starved soldiers had not seen action in Hungary since Suleyman's campaign of 1566. By Peçevi's reckoning, the numbers of combatants amassing on the Hungarian border was exceptionally large, including thirty thousand Rumelian troops and as many imperial household troops. In particular, noted Peçevi, furloughed soldiers and freebooters were pressing for an opportunity to reap booty; their numbers equaled the Rumelians. The Tatar Han, an ally of the Ottomans, estimated 150,000 in total, though Peçevi thought it was closer to 120,000 combatants.[9] He judged that the massed troops could have raided and plundered all the way to Prague.

The commander in charge, Sinan Pasha (no favorite of Peçevi), had at first held back his men, reasoning that if fighters were let loose, the land would be despoiled, and nothing would be left for the Ottoman state to tax. But then he changed his mind, now saying "if you want to incorporate a new land into your domains, you may have to suffer damage to the one you march through to get there." The pasha put no limits on the conduct of the invasion—"no restriction, no cautions." Peçevi was particularly distressed that peasants and their families would be taken captive and villages destroyed by fire. He also noted, with a touch of despair, that young volunteers who had distinguished themselves in combat had turned to raiding their fellow combatants. They charged at night from the safety of the earthen fortifications they themselves had constructed. Peçevi had nearly been one of their victims, which prompted him to sleep at night with his musket at his side.

A few years before the Hungarian operation, developments at the other end of the empire had preoccupied Peçevi, although this time he was not reporting as eye-witness.[10] In 1585, with their principal theater of war having shifted to the Caucasus, the Ottomans retook Tabriz, the capital city of the historical region of Azerbaijan. It had been the first major conquest, in 1501, of the Iranian Safavids. Peçevi wrote with both reservation and admiration about two military confrontations that took place in the years following the Ottoman victory. The protagonists were Cafer Pasha, the powerful but somewhat erratic Ottoman governor newly appointed to Tabriz, and the soldiers who served him. Peçevi described two incidents, one in which plunder was selfishly denied, the other a jubilee of shared booty. If Peçevi had a cause, it was fairness in sharing the spoils of victory.

Peçevi's first story concerned an event that took place a year after the Ottoman conquest. Having replaced Ferhad Pasha, the victor at Tabriz, Cafer needed a *huruç*, a major exploit in his new office. He chose the city of Güherdan, a local Persian capital situated on the route to Ottoman-controlled Baghdad. Although "ghazis" from Tabriz raided three or four times a month, the city appeared unconquerable. Cafer Pasha's opportunity finally came when the sultan of Güherdan failed in his own attempt to recover Tabriz, with the aim of wiping out "the Turks." Taking immediate advantage of the sultan's disgrace (he had failed to seek the shah's permission), Cafer attacked and won his battle.

Peçevi's only comment on this episode was "the fact is, he appropriated all [the spoils] for himself." Rewards for the troops would have to wait. However, Peçevi would chronicle the deteriorating relationship over the next couple of years between Cafer and the soldiers. The increasing tension and then reprisals between them escalated to the point that Cafer was plotting to massacre the troops. Peçevi called the prolonged episode "an event utterly unheard of in the whole world's history of sovereigns."

95

As much as Cafer relished a good battle, Peçevi liked a good story. He found an opportunity in the events of 1590, as the pasha planned a campaign against Persian lords in the vicinity of Tabriz. As Peçevi reported it, the latter were reluctant to face the Ottomans, until the moment Cafer goaded them into action. He dispatched a taunting message: "If you were men, you could accomplish more." The Persians' response was to send Cafer various battle accoutrements plus a colorful kerchief along with the message, "If you are a man, then face us wearing these [gift items]; if you don't come, then sit in a corner and spin with your spinning top." Cafer reciprocated with a carafe, a drinking cup, and manly clothing, along with a message saying "Enjoy yourselves! With God's support, we will oppose you. I doubt you'll be spinning."[11]

This verbal jousting apparently incited "a thousand Turkish braves" eager for combat. The Ottoman forces pursued the Persians across the river and up into the highlands to which they had withdrawn. As Peçevi narrated it, the following three days and three nights were "beyond description." In the end, the Ottoman soldiers' efforts culminated in the seizure of the enemy encampment.

Following his positive account of the soldiers' performance, Peçevi turned to the plunder to which they were now entitled. As he put it, "they settled into [the business] of complete gratification." The booty that "became the property of the ghazis of Islam" included "silver-complected odalisques" and "Circassian youths, each one with a full-moon face, his beauty at its peak." Fifteen select captives and exceptionally precious objects had been sent to the sultan. In response, Cafer Pasha received a *ferman* promoting him to the rank of vezir, along with a sword adorned with gold and two magnificent caftans. For Peçevi, who did not always approve of the act of plunder, this had been a significant as well as successful victory. The rewards in booty were licit.

* * *

Military officers could wreak havoc without leaving their home base. Such was the case of Halil Beg, a cavalryman in the city of Harput who committed one outrage after another. He was no common brigand, however, but rather a member of the garrison stationed in the ancient fortress of Harput, a provincial capital in eastern Anatolia. In 1632, the Harput judge recorded the cavalryman's multiple abuses as testified to by a wide range of residents both from the city and the province's villages. However, other entries by the Harput judge suggest that this knotty legal case had deeper roots and ramifications. Court records were not always a transparent representation of events.[12]

Twenty-one individuals came before the judge to protest the violence done to them or their family. Testimony came from the prominent and the obscure, Muslim and Christian, women and men. A sample of eight testimonies follows, in the order in which the judge inscribed them in the joint complaint:

- Kasap Hasan Ağa: The brothers Cafer and Hüseyin and also Mevlud, all sent by] the aforementioned Halil Beg, broke into my house and beat me severely inside my house for no reason. Moreover they [twisted my turban around my neck] and carried me away from the entrance to the judge's court [but] Muslims [men of good repute] drew round and rescued me.

- Seyyid Abu Bekr: Despite the fact that I hold the office of city steward by the most noble and honorable patent [of the sultan], Yusuf Çelebi, one of the followers of the aforementioned Halil Beg, took over the stewardship; and because I said "the sultan's edict is the law," they cursed me vituperatively.

- Osman son of Mehmed Beşe [Beşe was a military rank]: The aforementioned Halil Beg, on a winter

98

day, forcibly seized my house, which is worth 200 kurush; overpowering me by force, he dumped a few coins on top of me. He committed violence and injustice toward me.

- The [female] city-dweller Nurcan, a Christian: The aforementioned Halil sent [his] men and they raided my house and broke down five of my doors one by one, and they seized my brother's son Kesbir and made him his [Halil's] boy, and they plundered like a horde [of ignorant beasts of prey].[13]

- Nurcan's daughter Yeşecan: The aforementioned Halil Beg sent his men, and they raided my house and seized my young son, and they broke down the doors of seven other houses.

- The villagers of [Nermeşbend]: The aforementioned Halil Beg sent Kızıl Rumi Beg, one of his followers, to collect our taxes; he took two horses and a gratuity of 20 kurush. We have yet to be saved [from him].

- Mir Haci son of Arslan: The aforementioned Halil Beg gets together with several brigands, who are his followers, to hang out and drink right next to my houses. One winter day, he forcibly and violently evicted my [servants] and my family from my house and occupied my houses and added them to his own [stock of] houses.

- The wife of Kıtbaş Gâvur: The aforementioned Halil Beg sent Ümmitzade Yusuf Beg; he seized my son Murad, claiming that his father owed him [Halil] some money, and they sold him [into captivity].

Finally, speaking again, now in one voice, this mixed group of urban and village residents cited the irregularities in taxation:

All during his time here, he has taken a gratuity for opening new wells. In violation of Sharia and imperial law, he takes two kurush per village well and one kurush for each city well. [Halil had been collecting taxes since 1628.]

Following this litany of abuses, the last speakers (possibly the entire group of complainants) summarized the irregularities they had just detailed and then presented their demand for a response from leading figures in the province:

Now it is our request that the oppression and tyranny that the aforementioned Halil Beg has visited upon us and the circumstances of these events and all the instances of oppression and tyranny that have been cited be investigated . . . and [the response] recorded [by the judge].[14]

Validation came the next day, when a group of respondents, largely members of Harput's civilian and military elites, testified that the previous day's allegations were legitimate:

Until the present time, the aforementioned soldier named Halil Beg and his men have killed four or five men with no justification, and he raids houses and abducts boys, and he has committed in excess all the oppression and tyranny cited above toward both Muslims and non-Muslims. There is no dissent among them on this point." The tax offenses were ignored in this response, and the respondents appear to somewhat distance themselves from the plaintiffs [among *them*].

The repetition of the refrain "oppression and tyranny" by both accusers and respondents was a deliberate choice of vocabulary. It had the effect of heightening the tenor of the accusations against Halil Beg. The phrase signaled the speakers' determination to pursue some form of aid or restitution. It had become a buzzword in formal complaints, especially those from stricken populations. The fact that the Harput complainants employed the slogan twice and the respondents repeated it suggests that the collective testimony could be useful in any future treatment of Halil's case. It was a catalogue of crimes and a portrait of a community at constant risk.

The final entry in the Harput court register included another summary statement of Halil's crimes, more emphatic and longer. It was likely the judge's summary:

> The soldier named Halil Beg, son of Küçük Haci Mustafa Beşe, one of the cavalrymen residing in the district of Harput, treats us with great oppression and tyranny such that nothing like this has ever happened before. Evil practices have appeared: for the tax on wells, he takes one akçe per city well and two akçes per village well. And while [it] is forbidden, he takes from the poor one and a half bushels from every [measure] of grain. Because of the oppression and injustice of the aforementioned, many people have fled and are in a state of ruination. Moreover, he has raided houses and abducted young boys and has caused many husbands to

repudiate their wives.[15] And he has conspired with the tax-collectors who come . . . and has collected taxes where there should be none. He spares no occasion for oppression and tyranny. It is our request that the notables of the province be questioned concerning the state of affairs regarding the aforementioned, and that [their response] be recorded.

Unlike the second entry, this one speaks for both the original complainants and the community as a whole. It is noteworthy that the emphasis here is on Halil's fraudulent tax claims, a crime that threatened not only the province's residents but also the imperial fisc. The statement also introduces a second staple in the rhetoric of appeal—the disaster of families fleeing their now untenable homes and falling into poverty. The phrase *perişan ve perakende*, "wretched and scattered from one another," was a buzzword in such records of complaint. If the court session had been an open one, listeners might remember neighbors who had fled and hope they themselves would be saved from the same fate. For the state, the consequences were loss of productive labor and a decline in tax revenue. The catchword was a powerful one, the consequence of "oppression and tyranny." Were further contention to occur in Harput and a petition to higher-ups be drafted, these linked phrases would doubtless appear.

103

* * *

How did things come to such a pass in Harput? For one thing, its geography played a role. Harput was less integrated into Ottoman systems of government than were central, western, and even southeaster Anatolian provinces. In addition, labelling Harput "eastern Anatolian" is somewhat misleading, given that "the east" was a vast and ambiguous stretch of territory. Erzurum and Diyarbakir, the two easternmost military bastions, did not face the territories of the rival Safavids or the potential designs of Caucasian powers—rather, they fronted a vast no-man's-land punctuated with relatively isolated urban centers.

The last war that had brought imperial power to the vicinity of Harput had been Suleyman's campaign against Iran. Begun in August 1553, the long conflict ended in a draw and formally concluded only in spring 1555, when a peace treaty was finally confirmed.[16] The scope of this campaign was nothing like those Suleyman led in Europe, which typically lasted four to eight months. Nor did it resemble the accomplishments of the pashas Ferhad and Cafer in the Tabriz region, despite their important wins. No other imperial campaign would cross Anatolia to the east until Murad IV set out in 1635, some eighty years after Suleyman. Meanwhile, the brilliant Shah Abbas had been recovering territories lost to the Ottomans in eastern Anatolia, the Caucasus, and Mesopotamia.

Before the actual campaign, Murat and his advisers would familiarize themselves with the terrain they would traverse by gathering advance intelligence. In addition to military goals, the long marches from one halt to the next provided opportunity for the sultan and his leading men to acquaint themselves with local conditions. As they made camp along their route, they could also convene with local officials. Fortress cities were especially opportune sites, useful when a large army quartered its forces in more than one location: during Suleyman's eastern campaigns, he wintered with some of his troops in Aleppo, while other contingents were stationed in the environs of Damascus, Tripoli, Amman, and Antioch. As for Harput, whether or not it was on the imperial route, early rumors of an eastern campaign would no doubt spur its community leaders to address the province's administrative health.

It is possible, even likely, that the Harput investigation and its censuring of Halil were generated in the run-up to Murad's eastern campaign. However, a look at Harput's earlier administrative history suggests that Halil's career as an urban brigand was not an extraordinary situation. A change in Harput's administrative status in the late sixteenth century had expanded opportunities for graft. The province was converted from one divided into military fiefs into a tax farm. In the former, taxes were collected by locally assigned agents and remitted to the imperial treasury, whereas in the latter, the "farmer" and his men collected and remitted the tax revenues.

If this new system produced greater revenue or the more assiduous collection of taxes, it was detrimental to the taxpayers. The Harput tax farm in this period was typically under the control of the provincial governor, who "owned" the farm. One such governor, Mehmed Beg, was dismissed when he scammed the local populace: he created a monopoly on crops whose sale price he was able to manipulate by stockpiling the crops when they were collected as tax in kind. Despite his dismissal, Mehmed reacquired the tax farm six weeks later, on the condition that he compensate the injured farmers.[17] He was succeeded by others like him, underlining the challenge to Istanbul of controlling the management of distant provinces.

Mehmed's successor was no better. Mahmud so abused the local population that they lodged a "severe complaint" against him. He had forced sales of grain at 180 percent of the going price and cotton at more than 200 percent. At the same time, he extorted cash from villagers who refused to buy. It took the governors-general of Erzurum and Diyarbakır, the judge and new governor of Harput, and the Imperial Council in Istanbul to bring him down. "This is the custom and the rule in these parts" was his retort. A subsequent holder of the office, Alaeddin, purchased the tax farm governorship, which he had contracted in exchange for 200,000 gold pieces. However, when he lagged in paying the Imperial Treasury, Istanbul instructed the Diyarbakır governor-general to make him pay up or else imprison him in the Diyarbakır fortress.

The degree of insubordination displayed by Harput governors underlines the challenges of managing distant provinces, especially those with significant military installations. Intertwined with Harput's political history was its surrounding environment. A useful contrast is the province of Aintab, conquered by the Ottomans a year after Harput.[18] Aintab was situated in a region densely populated by cities and towns and crisscrossed with trade routes. Oversight by the governorate-general to which it belonged came from a neighboring city (close enough that a villager could take their suit to the governor-general themselves). Harput by contrast was relatively isolated, providing its leading figures more leeway to deviate from administrative norms and imperial policy.

Had Halil been a rogue operator until the populace of Harput could no longer endure his menacing conduct? Or were he and his posse handmaid to one or more persons in higher authority in Harput? Were the excessive tax revenues turned over to a bona fide fiscal authority or shared among a coterie of garrison leaders? Who would become the owners of the boys who were abducted and the dwellings that were seized? The court investigations neatly pinned Halil Beg as the author of the multiple crimes. If the legal activity had been generated with the anticipation of Murad IV's campaign in mind, the ready answer would already be inscribed in the court record. Three attestations of Halil's guilt constituted the paper trail of a seemingly just administration. Then again, Harput could be answerable to higher authorities, beginning with the two eastern governorates-general and perhaps ending with the sultan.

* * *

It should be clear by now that not everyone feared bandits or extortionists. They were sometimes fixers, men who could serve those in power or perform legally condemned acts for the benefit of clients. Moreover, there could be appealing elements of romance and daring in tales of banditry or seizure of captives—recall Peçevi's observation that people tended to admire a successful outlaw and even go so far as to shelter him.

In 1554, Suleyman's subjects, pressing him to seize a member of the rival Safavid dynasty, had perhaps not considered that the same catastrophe could strike the Ottomans. The sultan's two-year absence on the Iranian front had demonstrated the risks of expansionist ambitions. In these same years, however, Suleyman was becoming known as "the Lawgiver." Around 1540, he and his legal staff had begun to crack down on abductions perpetrated within the empire by prescribing the dire penalty of castration for captors and their accomplices. Likewise, females, who had been tacitly assumed by the law to be victims, could now be viewed as accomplices. In other words, acts of abduction were being defined as both a public menace and a crime to obliterate.

As if in reaction, the uses of abduction as a public assertion of power, even valor, began to be appropriated by opponents of the government's vision of order. Tellingly, it was in this period that tales of the bandit-hero Köroğlu ("son of the blind man") began to take hold among the Ottomans. A Robin Hood-like outlaw, Köroğlu was the celebrated subject of popular tales that were often set in northwestern Anatolia.[19] The fact that his legend emerged in a heyday of brigandage prompts questions about the honorable uses of violence and resistance—namely, whether the "crimes" of the abductor-outlaw might also be seen as a justifiable response to misgovernment. What pushes Köroğlu into a life of banditry is the unjust blinding of his father by the local governor, who had employed the father as his equerry. This event casts both father and son into poverty. The anti-hero of injustice in Köroğlu tales is often Bolu Bey, the governor of Bolu, a forested mountain region northwest of Ankara. Sometimes however, the antagonist is the Ottoman sultan, who in any case is ultimately responsible for the father's incapacitation. Certainly, Köroğlu is rendered more admirable than the authorities who blinded a man who served them.

Perhaps predictably, the legends conspicuously recounted Köroğlu's own abductions. His love and longing drive his kidnapping of Ayvaz, the son of a butcher. Köroğlu is also depicted in acts of abducting one or more females, typically daughters of magnates. It is not a great a stretch to suggest parallels in Suleyman's associations with his most prized captive servants. The sultan's longtime grand vezir Ibrahim, son of an Ionian fisherman, was also his boon companion. Suleyman endowed Ibrahim with both great authority and great wealth (he was said to have over a thousand slaves of his own). The vezir's end came when he was executed in 1536 for having defied imperial orders and lost a key battle, jeopardizing the eastern front. More influential in the long run was Hurrem,

Suleyman's favorite concubine, who had been abducted from today's Ukraine. He not only bestowed riches and power on her, but also shocked his subjects by making her the only Ottoman concubine to marry her master. The sultan's public found both these attachments troubling as well as bewildering.

One might say of both Suleyman and Köroğlu that they were honorable abductors who did not abuse their victims. Indeed, it could be argued that they were humanized by them. Of Köroğlu it has been said that it was because his barren wife longs for a son that he abducts the boy Ayvaz. Today he is remembered both as a hero who fought for justice and a notable bandit. Suleyman composed copious poetry for and about his beloved Hurrem. As for the Ottoman sultans' forceable use of their foreign captives, especially those who governed alongside them, it was hardly unique in the broad and ancient history of the region.

Royal figures might themselves fall victim to captors, most humiliatingly to other royalty. For example, there was Timur's capture and incarceration of Sultan Bayezid I in 1402 and Selim I's seizure of the daughter of an Iranian shah. Even as late as 1554, Hurrem was sending urgent messages to Suleyman on the frontier, warning him that his subjects would cheer him only if the shah's wife or son was captured. Some were even wondering whether the sultan was still fit to command.

Illustrious figures were indeed highly valued conquests. Some might be paraded at court as the empire's prized captives, for example, Alqas Mirza, a dissident brother of Tahmasp I, the shah of Iran. Others, new prisoners of war, became strategic additions to the Ottomans' extant fighting forces and helped to broadcast the strength of the empire's military capacity. Once trained, these new recruits could conceivably be ordered by the sultan and his commanders to turn around and fight their native countrymen. Forcing countrymen to slay each other was only one of the fundamental conundrums that could be met along the spectrum of captivity.

Notes

Preface

[1] *The Return of Martin Guerre* (original French: *Le Retour de Martin Guerre*) is a 1982 film directed by Daniel Vigne starring Gérard Depardieu. Its plot is based on a case of imposture in sixteenth-century France.
[2] "Past Perfect with Leslie Peirce," CEU Medieval Radio, *Past Perfect!* https://medievalradio.org/2018/10/15/past-perfect-with-leslie-peirce-now-available/

Chapter 1

[1] Sahillioğlu, "Slaves," 134.
[2] Aintab Sicili 2: 23b.
[3] Seng, "Fugitives," 154–55.
[4] Inalcik, "Servile Labor," 35.
[5] Sahillioğlu, "Slaves," 127ff.
[6] Sobers-Khan, *Shackles.*
[7] White, *Piracy,* 4 and passim.
[8] D 8030, f. 1bB.
[9] Seng, "Fugitives," 204.
[10] Seng, "Liminal," 36–37.
[11] Lewis, *Istanbul,* 102–103.
[12] Peirce, *Empress,* 240.
[13] The highest ranking of the state-owned kul lived in extreme luxury, attended by legions of their own household slaves. The most prominent kul domicile in this period was the Istanbul palace first owned by the grand vizier Ibrahim Pasha, who served Suleyman I, "the Magnificent" from 1523 until his death in 1536 (today it serves as the Turkish and Islamic Arts Museum).
[14] Wilkins, *Solidarities,* 292.
[15] Hanna, *Big Money,* 65.
[16] Ibid., 156.
[17] Düzdağ, *Fetvalar,* 55. The fatwa referred to Jewish and Christian women as "infidels."

[18] Imber, *Empire*, 120.

[19] Soucek, *Memoirs*, 97.

[20] Erdem, *Slavery*, 6, ft. 24, 25.

[21] İnalcık, *Suret-i Defter*.

[22] Sahillioğlu, "Slaves," 132.

[23] Soucek, *Maritime Wars*, 32.

[24] İnalcık, "Servile Labor," 32–34.

[25] Weiss, *Captives*, 217n9.

[26] For an example of an elaborate prisoner swap initiated by an Ottoman mother, see White, *Piracy*, 78.

[27] Qur'an, 9:60.

[28] David & Fodor, *Ransom Slavery*, passim.

[29] Aintab Sicili 161: 28c.

[30] Note that slaves could be freed at any time, not only at particular life moments.

[31] Sahillioğlu, "Slaves," 113.

[32] Aintab Sicili 2: 127a, 262a, 289b.

[33] Aintab Sicili 161: 95a; Düzdağ, *Fetvalar*, 153 (#745).

[34] Ongan, *Ankara*, #1274.

[35] İnalcık, "Servile Labor," 33–34.

[36] Ongan, *Ankara*, #514 (Ferhad), #1411 (Şirmerd).

[37] Sahillioğlu, "Slaves", 119.

[38] Imber, *Empire*, 130.

[39] While I was doing dissertation research in the Topkapı Palace Archive in 1985, an elderly gentleman from Trabzon came to consult the Trabzon court records for a property deed from Ottoman times. (At the time, court records were not yet centralized in Ankara's National Library, with the exception of Istanbul's vast collections.)

Chapter 2

[1] Koçlar, "362 Harput Şer'iyye Sicili," 171–72.

[2] Roth, *Law Collections*, 291, #12.

[3] Dig. 1. 18.13 (*De officio praesidiis*), quoted by Shaw, "Bandits," 14; 16.

[4] Akgündüz, *Kanunnameler*, 2:42–43.

[5] This punishment was imposed by the then Grand Vezir Lutfi Pasha, it caused a disagreement with his princess wife, who divorced him when he struck her in the heat of argument.

[6] Crawford, *European Sexualities*, 157.

[7] See chapter 1 for timariots, cavalrymen appointed to rural fiefs.

[8] See Heyd, *Ottoman Documents*, for the Dulkadir Kanunname.

[9] Mühimme Register No. 3, Case 455.

[10] Mühimme Register No. 3, Case 560.

[11] Mühimme Register No. 3, Case 672.

[12] Mühimme Register No. 3, Case 196.

[13] Heyd, *Ottoman Documents*, 132.

[14] Shaw, "Bandits"

[15] The Dulkadir administrative center was Maraş, some 80 kilometers (50 miles) from Antep city, while Aleppo was 120 kilometers (75 miles) distant.

[16] Peirce, *Morality Tales*, 302–304.

[17] İnalcık, *Economic*, 127 and passim.

[18] Özdeğer, *Ayintab Livası*, 377–78.

[19] Peirce, *Morality Tales*, 304–305.

[20] İnalcık, *Economic,* 120–29.

[21] Mühimme Register No. 3, Case 880.

[22] Mühimme Register No. 3, Case 1359.

[23] AS 151: 5C. Villagers could be liable for crimes committed on village lands.

[24] AS 2: 117a.

[25] İnalcık, *Economic*, 126–27.

[26] Qur'an 9:60.

[27] Millar, *Roman Near East*, 248–49.

[28] Güzelbey, *Evliyalar*, 21.

[29] Evliya Çelebi, *Seyahatname*, 9:359; in Evliya's version, Dülük Baba is still alive when the sultan returns.

[30] Terms of opprobrium found in the 1630–1631 Register of Important Affairs (*Mühimme Defteri*) include şaki/eşkıya [eşkıya is the plural

of şaki, but was used as a singular noun as well], *ehl-i fesad, zalim/za-lemen, te'addi [eden], fırkatacı, haramî, haramzade, 'âsi, eşirra*; also *levend [taifesi], sekban eşkıyası*, and even *sekban eşkıya levendi*. For a useful discussion of historiographical typologies of the bandit, see Barkey, *Bandits and Bureaucrats*, 176ff.

[31] Mühimme Register No. 85 (1040–1041/1630–1631), Order #381 (3 June 1631), 232–33.

[32] In stating the size of a band of brigands, the registers typically estimate a range, e.g., four to five, thirty to forty, here forty to fifty, and so on. Forty may be a trope for a good-sized band (as in the tale of Ali Baba and the forty thieves).

Chapter 3

[1] Fetvacı, *Picturing History*, 17.

[2] Fetvacı, *Picturing History*, 39; see also p. 200.

[3] Topkapı Sarayı Müsesi Arşivi, E. 5038.

[4] Peirce, *Imperial Harem*, 37.

[5] Neşri, *Kitâb-ı Cihan-Nüma*, I: 68–81.

[6] Ibn Kemal, *Tevarih-i Al-ı Osman*, Book 1.

[7] Akgunduz, *Kanunlar*, II: 135.

[8] *Ghazi* is a term for a Muslim soldier when he is fighting against non-Muslims. Now that Osman has become a ruler, the term is justified.

[9] Peçevi, *Peçevi Tarihi*, Vol. 2, 144–45.

[10] Peçevi, *Peçevi Tarihi*, 104ff.

[11] Peçevi, *Peçevi Tarihi*.

[12] The court record is found in Harput Şeriye Sicili, 181, page 11, case 1. (I thank the Islam Araştırma Merkezi [Center for Research on Islam] in Istanbul for furnishing me with a Xerox copy of the Harput court record.)

[13] Door (*kapu*) may indicate individual units in a multiple-unit dwelling.

[14] The people's "request" (*sual olunub sicil olunması matlub*ımızdır) could also be translated as "demand."

[15] The implication is that the women have been abducted and raped,

and then, by common custom, divorced by their husbands. The absence in the first case record of allegations that wives were abducted is noteworthy; perhaps the husbands wished to avoid a public record of their dishonor.

[16] October 1554 onward was spent in part waiting for Safavid negotiators to arrive in Amasya for the drafting of a tready.

[17] This account of Harput's governors is drawn from Ünal, *Harput Sancağı*, which extends beyond the sixteenth century, despite the book's title.

[18] See chapter 2 for a look at Aintab.

[19] Many versions of Köroğlu tales can be found in Caucasian and other Turkic languages; the Anatolian cycle itself has numerous variations.

117

Bibliography

Please note that the bibliography is somewhat handicapped as it was assembled during the months when my university's library and faculty offices have been closed due to the COVID-19 pandemic, making some books listed inaccessible.

PRIMARY SOURCES

Aintab Sicilleri, Nos. 2, 161. Milli Kütüphane, Ankara. Gaziantep Sharia Court Record, National Library, Ankara.

Aşıkpaşazade Tevarih-i Al-i Osman (Aşıkpaşazade Tarihi) [Annals of the House of Osman] Istanbul: Matbaa-i âmire, 1913 [1332].

D8030. Başbakanlık Osmanlı Arşivi. Register 8030, Prime Ministry Ottoman Archive.

Çelebi Evliya. *Evliya Çelebi Seyahatnamesi* [Evliya Çelebi's book of travels, book 9]. Edited and translated by Yücel Dağlı et. al. Istanbul: Yapı Kredi Yayınları, 2003.

"Dulkadir Kanunname" [Dulkadir lawbook]. In Uriel Heyd, *Ottoman Documents on Palestine 1552–1651: A Study of the Firman according to the Mühimme Defteri.* Oxford: Clarendon Press, 1982.

Harput Şeriye Sicili No. 3. [Harput court record no. 3]. Xerox copy courtesy of the Islam Araştırma Merkezi (Center for Research on Islam, Istanbul).

Inalcık, Halil, ed. *Hicri 835 Tarihli Suret-i Defter-i Sancak-ı Arnavid* [Copy of the register of the district of Arnavid (Albania), dated 845 Hijri]. Ankara: Türk Tarih Kurumu Basımevi, 1954.

Neşri, Mehmed. *Kitab-ı Cihan-Nüma (Neşri Tarihi), 1. Cilt.* [The book of the world-sheltering (Sultan): Neşri's history, book one]. Edited by Faik Reşat Unat and Mehmed A. Köymen. Ankara: Türk Tarih Kurumu Basımevi, 1987.

Oruç Beg Tarihi [Oruç Beg's history]. Edited by Necdet Öztürk. Istanbul: Çamlıca Basım Yayın Kitaplar No. 36, 2008.

Peçevi, Ibrahim Efendi, *Peçevi Tarihi* [Peçevi's history]. Vol. 2. Edited by Bekir Sıtkı Baykal. Ankara: Kültür ve Turizm Bakanlığı Yayınları, 1982.

Kemalpaşazade, Şemseddin Ahmed. *Tevarih-i Al-ı Osman, I. Defter* [Histories of the House of Osman, Book 1]. Edited by Şerafettin Turan. Ankara: Türk Tarih Kurumu Basımevi, 1970.

Mühimme Register No. 3. *3 Numaralı Mühimme Defteri, 966–968* [Register of important affairs, No. 3, 1558–1560]. Ankara: T.C. Başbakanlık Devlet Arşivleri Genel Müdürlüğü, 1993.

Mühimme Register No. 85. *85 Numaralı Mühimme Defteri (1040–1041/1630–1631)* [Register of important affairs 85, 1630–1631]. Ankara: Devlet Arşivleri Genel Müdürlüğü, Osmanlı Arşivi Daire Başkanlığı, 2002.

Koçlar, Bekir. "362 Numaralı Harput Şer`iyye Sicili" [Harput Sharia court record, no. 362.] Transliterated and analyzed by Bekir Koçlar. MA Thesis, Fırat University, 1990. T.C. Yüksek Öğretim Kurulu Dokümantasyon Merkezi.

SECONDARY SOURCES

Akgündüz, Ahmed. *Osmanlı Kanunnameleri ve Hukuki Tahlilleri* [Ottoman Law codes and their Judicial Analysis]. Vol. 1. Istanbul: Osmanlı Araştırmaları Vakfı, 1990.

Aydın, Bilgin, and Rıfat Günalan. *XV. ve XVI. Yüzyıllarda Osmanlı Maliye ve Defter Sistemi* [The Ottoman financial and treasury system]. Istanbul: Yeditepe Yayınları, 2008.

Barkey, Karen. *Bandits and Bureaucrats: The Ottoman Route to State Centralization.* Ithaca, NY: Cornell University Press, 1994.

Crawford, Katherine. *European Sexualities, 1400–1800.* Cambridge: Cambridge University Press, 2007.

Dávid, Géza, and Pál Fodor. *Ransom Slavery along the Ottoman Borders: Early Fifteen–Early Eighteenth Centuries.* Leiden–Boston: Brill, 2007.

Düzdağ, M. Ertuğrul. Şeyhülislam *Ebussuud Efendi Fetvaları Işığında 19: Asır Türk Hayatı* [Turkish Life as Illuminated by the Fatwas of Sheikh ul-Islam Ebussuud Efendi]. Istanbul: Enderun Kitabevi, 1983.

Erdem, Y. Hakan. *Slavery in the Ottoman Empire and Its Demise, 1800–1909.* New York: Palgrave McMillan, 1996.

Fetvaçı, Emine. *Picturing History at the Ottoman Court.* Bloomington and Indianapolis: Indiana University Press, 2013.

Güzelbey, Cemil Cahit. *Gaziantep Evliyaları* [The Mystics of Gaziantep]. Gaziantep: Gaziantep Kültür Yayınları, 1966.

Hanna, Nelly. *Making Big Money in 1660: The Life and Times of Isma'il Abu Taqiyya, Egyptian Merchant.* Syracuse, NY: Syracuse University Press, 1998.

Heyd, Uriel. *Ottoman Documents on Palestine 1552–1615: A Study of the Firman according to the Mühimme Defteri.* Oxford: Clarendon Press, 1960.

Imber, Colin. *The Ottoman Empire, 1300–1650: The Structure of Power.* New York: Palgrave McMillan, 2020.

İnalcık, Halil. "Servile Labor in the Ottoman Empire." In *Studies in Ottoman Social and Economic History*, 25–52. London: Variorum Reprints, 1985.

İnalcık, Halil, with Donald Quataert, eds. *An Economic and Social History of the Ottoman Empire.* Vol. 1, 1300–1914. Cambridge: Cambridge University Press, 1994.

Lewis, Bernard. *Istanbul and the Civilization of the Ottoman Empire.* (Centers of Civilization vol. 9) Norman: University of Oklahoma Press, 1963.

Millar, Fergus. *The Roman Near East 31 BC–AD 337.* Cambridge MA: Harvard University Press, 1993.

Ongan, Halit. *Ankara'nın İki Numaralı Şer'iye Sicili* [Ankara's No. 2 Court Record]. Ankara: TürK Tarih Kurumu Basımevi, 1974.

Özdeğer, Hüseyin. *Onaltıncı Asırda Ayintab Livası*, Vol. 1. [The Province of Ayintab in the Sixteenth Century]. Istanbul: Bayrak Matbacılık, 1988.

Peirce, Leslie. *Morality Tales: Law and Gender in the Ottoman Court of Aintab.* Berkeley: University of California Press, 2003.

———. *Empress of the East: How a European Slave Girl Became Queen of the Ottoman Empire.* New York: Basic Books, 2017.

121

Roth, Martha T. *Law Collections from Mesopotamia and Asia Minor.* (Society of Biblical Literature Writings from the Ancient World 6.) Atlanta, GA: Society of Biblical Literature–Scholars Press, 1997.

Sahillioğlu, Halil. "Slaves in the Social and Economic Life of Bursa in the Late 15th and Early 16th Centuries." *Turcica* 17 (1985): 43–112.

Seng, Yvonne. "Invisible Women: Residents of Early Sixteenth-Century Istanbul." In *Women in the Medieval Islamic World*, edited by Gavin R. G. Hambly, 24–68. Basingstoke: Palgrave Macmillan/New York: St. Martin's Press, 1998.

————. "Fugitives and Factotums: Slaves in Early Sixteenth-Century Istanbul." *Journal of the Economic and Social History of the Orient* 39, no. 2 (1996): 136–69.

————. "A Liminal State: Slavery in Sixteenth-Century Istanbul." In *Slavery in the Islamic Middle East*, edited by Shaun E. Marmon, 25–42. Princeton, NJ: Marcus Weiner Publishers, 1999.

Shaw, Brent D. "Bandits in the Roman Empire." *Past and Present* 105, no. 1 (Nov. 1984): 3–52.

Sobers-Khan, Nur. *Slaves without Shackles: Forced Labour and Manumission in the Galata Court Registers, 1560–1572* (Studien Zur Sprache, Geschichte Und Kultur der Turkvölker 29.) Berlin: Klaus Schwarz Verlag, 2014.

Ünal, Mehmet Ali. *XVI Yüzyılda Harput Sancağı (1518–1566)* [The Province of Harput in the 16th century, 1518–1566]. Ankara: Türk Tarih Kurumu Basımevi, 1989.

Weiss, Gillian. *Captives and Corsairs: France and Slavery in the Early Modern Mediterranean.* Stanford, CA: Stanford University Press, 2011.

White, Joshua M. *Piracy and Law in the Ottoman Mediterranean.* Stanford, CA: Stanford University Press, 2017.

Wilkins, Charles. *Forging Urban Solidarities: Ottoman Aleppo 1640–1700.* Leiden–Boston: Brill, 2009.

Index